August 1935

MODERN
ENGLISH ESSAYS

EDITED BY ERNEST RHYS

W.H. CAFFYN.

Austin Dobson

MODERN
ENGLISH ESSAYS
VOLUME TWO

E.C. STEDMAN
ANDREW LANG
EDMUND GOSSE
AUSTIN DOBSON
R. L. STEVENSON
AUGUSTINE BIRRELL
RICHARD JEFFERIES
RICHARD GARNETT
LESLIE STEPHEN
SAMUEL BUTLER
H. C. BEECHING
JOHN W. HALES
G. RADFORD

1922
LONDON & TORONTO
J. M. DENT & SONS LTD.
NEW YORK: E. P. DUTTON & CO.

EDITOR'S NOTE

Obiter Dicta, which in 1886 announced a new essayist, well in the tradition, yet original, and gifted with allusive, whimsical humour, supplies two essays in this collection. The first, that on Carlyle, is Mr. Birrell's own; the second, on Falstaff, is by his friend, the late George Radford. Leslie Stephen is seen in his less known, more personal vein in his essay from the *Cornhill Magazine*, for which he wrote from the year 1866 onwards. In the cycle also of personal diversions, Samuel Butler's " Ramblings in Cheapside " is a delicious instance of philosophical fantasy, with a scientific moral to the tale. It was first printed in the *Universal Review*, 1890. Mr. Edmund Gosse is presented under two aspects from his *Gossip in a Library*—writing with mischievous zest upon cats and their chroniclers, and with librarious critical assignment on Christopher Smart. Austin Dobson on John Gay and Andrew Lang on Edgar Poe were perfectly suited to those diverse authors, as issued formerly in the *Parchment Library* (1881–1882). They represent a particular mode of essay-writing with an eye to the man behind the book, much in vogue in their day.

The cult of the literary picturesque was a fashion with Lang, Dobson and Robert Louis Stevenson; and its tendency is to be seen in many pages of those writers and their contemporaries, as in one famous example by the last-named, where it culminates in a Skeltian England:

" Here is the inn with the red curtain, pipes, spittoons and eight-day clock; and there again is that impressive dungeon with the chains, which was so dull to colour. England, the hedge-row elms, the thin brick houses, windmills, glimpses of the navigable Thames—England, when at last I came to visit it, was only Skelt made evident."

For the conscious art of the literary wayfarer, who is of the town, yet delighted with the wild, what better example could be found than Robert Louis Stevenson's " Walking Tours " in this volume, which comes from *Virginibus Puerisque*? (1881). Professor Hales upon Edmund Spenser, the " Poets' Poet," wrote with the feeling of a specialist. His essay, Dr. Garnett's on " A Translator of Plato's *Republic*," and Dean Beeching's on Hugh Latimer, are all from the same source, and were first contributed to editions of those authors prepared for " Everyman."   E. R.

For permission to use copyright material in this volume, special acknowledgment is due to the Rt. Hon. Augustine Birrell for the essays on Carlyle and on Falstaff; to Mr. Edmund Gosse for the essays on " Cats " and on Christopher Smart; to Mr. Festing Jones and Mr. Jonathan Cape for Samuel Butler's " Ramblings in Cheapside," and to Messrs. Chatto and Windus and Messrs. Scribners for Stevenson's " Walking Tours." The other copyright items have been either acquired by the present publishers from the original holders, or reprinted from volumes already in their list.

CONTENTS

	PAGE
CARLYLE (*Rt. Hon. Augustine Birrell*)	1
GAY'S FABLES (*Austin Dobson*)	32
THE POETRY OF EDGAR ALLAN POE (*Andrew Lang*)	50
A CYNIC'S APOLOGY (*Leslie Stephen*) . . .	64
CATS (*Edmund Gosse*)	84
CHRISTOPHER SMART (*Edmund Gosse*) . . .	92
A BELT OF ASTEROIDS (*Edmund Clarence Stedman*)	104
FALSTAFF (*George Radford*)	141
RAMBLINGS IN CHEAPSIDE (*Samuel Butler*) . .	161
WALKING TOURS (*Robert Louis Stevenson*) . .	181
GOLDSMITH (*Austin Dobson*) . . .	193
A TRANSLATOR OF PLATO'S "REPUBLIC" (*Richard Garnett*)	215
HUGH LATIMER (*H. C. Beeching*) . . .	226
THE POETS' POET (*John W. Hales*) . .	241

MODERN ENGLISH ESSAYS

CARLYLE

By the Rt. Hon. Augustine Birrell

THE accomplishments of our race have of late become so varied, that it is often no easy task to assign him whom we would judge to his proper station among men; and yet, until this has been done, the guns of our criticism cannot be accurately levelled, and as a consequence the greater part of our fire must remain futile. He, for example, who would essay to take account of Mr. Gladstone, must read much else besides Hansard; he must brush up his Homer, and set himself to acquire some theology. The place of Greece in the providential order of the world, and of laymen in the Church of England, must be considered, together with a host of other subjects of much apparent irrelevance to a statesman's life. So too in the case of his distinguished rival, whose death eclipsed the gaiety of politics and banished epigram from Parliament: keen must be the critical faculty which can nicely discern where the novelist ended and the statesman began in Benjamin Disraeli.

Happily, no such difficulty is now before us. Thomas Carlyle was a writer of books, and he was nothing else. Beneath this judgment he would have winced, but have remained silent, for the facts are so.

Little men sometimes, though not perhaps so often as is taken for granted, complain of their destiny, and think they have been hardly treated, in that they have been allowed to remain so undeniably small; but great men, with hardly an exception, nauseate their greatness, for not being of the particular sort they most fancy. The poet Gray was passionately fond, so his biographers tell us, of military history; but he took no Quebec. General Wolfe took Quebec, and whilst he was taking it, recorded the fact that he would sooner have written Gray's *Elegy*; and so Carlyle—who panted for action, who hated eloquence, whose heroes were Cromwell and Wellington, Arkwright and the "rugged Brindley," who beheld with pride and no ignoble envy the bridge at Auldgarth his mason-father had helped to build half a century before, and then exclaimed, "A noble craft, that of a mason; a good building will last longer than most books—than one book in a million"; who despised men of letters, and abhorred the "reading public"; whose gospel was Silence and Action—spent his life in talking and writing; and his legacy to the world is thirty-four volumes octavo.

There is a familiar melancholy in this; but the critic has no need to grow sentimental. We must have men of thought as well as men of action: poets as much as generals; authors no less than artisans; libraries at least as much as militia; and therefore we may accept and proceed critically to examine Carlyle's thirty-four volumes, remaining somewhat indifferent to the fact that had he had the fashioning of his own destiny, we should have had at his hands blows instead of books.

Taking him, then, as he was—a man of letters —perhaps the best type of such since Dr. Johnson died in Fleet Street, what are we to say of his thirty-four volumes?

In them are to be found criticism, biography, history, politics, poetry and religion. I mention this variety because of a foolish notion, at one time often found suitably lodged in heads otherwise empty, that Carlyle was a passionate old man, dominated by two or three extravagant ideas, to which he was for ever giving utterance in language of equal extravagance. The thirty-four volumes octavo render this opinion untenable by those who can read. Carlyle cannot be killed by an epigram, nor can the many influences that moulded him be referred to any single source. The rich banquet his genius has spread for us is of many courses. The fire and fury of the *Latter-Day Pamphlets* may be disregarded by the peaceful soul, and the preference given to the " Past " of *Past and Present*, which, with its intense and sympathetic mediævalism, might have been written

3

by a Tractarian. The *Life of Sterling* is the favourite book of many who would sooner pick oakum than read *Frederick the Great* all through; whilst the mere students of *belles lettres* may attach importance to the essays on Johnson, Burns, and Scott, on Voltaire and Diderot, on Goethe and Novalis, and yet remain blankly indifferent to *Sartor Resartus* and the *French Revolution*.

But true as this is, it is none the less true that, excepting possibly the *Life of Schiller*, Carlyle wrote nothing not clearly recognisable as his. All his books are his very own—bone of his bone, and flesh of his flesh. They are not stolen goods, nor elegant exhibitions of recently and hastily acquired wares.

This being so, it may be as well if, before proceeding any further, I attempt, with a scrupulous regard to brevity, to state what I take to be the invariable indications of Mr. Carlyle's literary handiwork—the tokens of his presence—" Thomas Carlyle, his mark."

First of all, it may be stated, without a shadow of a doubt, that he is one of those who would sooner be wrong with Plato than right with Aristotle; in one word, he is a mystic. What he says of Novalis may with equal truth be said of himself: " He belongs to that class of persons who do not recognise the syllogistic method as the chief organ for investigating truth, or feel themselves bound at all times to stop short where its light fails them. Many of his opinions he would despair of proving in the most patient court of law, and would remain well content that they should be disbelieved there." In philosophy we shall not be very far wrong if we rank Carlyle as a follower of Bishop Berkeley; for an idealist he undoubtedly was. "Matter," says he, "exists only spiritually, and to represent some idea, and body it forth. Heaven and Earth are but the time-vesture of the Eternal. The Universe is but one vast symbol of God; nay, if thou wilt have it, what is man himself but a symbol of God? Is not all that he does symbolical, a revelation to sense of the mystic Godgiven force that is in him? —a gospel of Freedom, which he, the 'Messias of Nature,' preaches as he can by act and word." "Yes, Friends," he elsewhere observes, "not our logical mensurative faculty, but our imaginative one, is King over us, I might say Priest and Prophet, to lead us heavenward, or magician and wizard to lead us hellward. The understanding is indeed thy window—too clear thou canst not make it; but phantasy is thy eye, with its colour-giving retina, healthy or diseased." It would be easy to multiply instances of this, the most obvious and interesting trait of Mr. Carlyle's writing; but I must bring my remarks upon it to a close by reminding you of his two favourite quotations, which have both significance. One from Shake-speare's *Tempest*:

> We are such stuff
> As dreams are made of, and our little life
> Is rounded with a sleep;

the other, the exclamation of the Earth-spirit, in Goethe's *Faust*:

'Tis thus at the roaring loom of Time I ply,
And weave for God the garment thou seest Him by.

But this is but one side of Carlyle. There is another as strongly marked, which is his second note; and that is what he somewhere calls "his stubborn realism." The combination of the two is as charming as it is rare. No one at all acquainted with his writings can fail to remember his almost excessive love of detail; his lively taste for facts, simply as facts. Imaginary joys and sorrows may extort from him nothing but grunts and snorts; but let him only worry out for himself, from that great dust-heap called "history," some undoubted fact of human and tender interest, and, however small it may be, relating possibly to some one hardly known, and playing but a small part in the events he is recording, and he will wax amazingly sentimental, and perhaps shed as many real tears as Sterne or Dickens do sham ones over their figments. This realism of Carlyle's gives a great charm to his histories and biographies. The amount he tells you is something astonishing— no platitudes, no rigmarole, no common-form, articles which are the staple of most biography, but, instead of them, all the facts and features of the case—pedigree, birth, father and mother, brothers and sisters, education, physiognomy, personal habits, dress, mode of speech; nothing escapes him. It was a characteristic criticism of his, on one of Miss Martineau's American books, that the story of the way Daniel Webster used to stand before the fire with his hands in his pockets was worth all the politics, philosophy, political economy, and sociology to be found in other portions of the good lady's writings. Carlyle's eye was indeed a terrible organ: he saw everything. Emerson, writing to him, says: "I think you see as pictures every street, church, Parliament-house, barracks, baker's shop, mutton-stall, forge, wharf, and ship, and whatever stands, creeps, rolls, or swims thereabout, and make all your own." He crosses over, one rough day, to Dublin; and he jots down in his diary the personal appearance of some unhappy creatures he never saw before or expected to see again; how men laughed, cried, swore, were all of huge interest to Carlyle. Give him a fact, he loaded you with thanks; propound a theory, you were rewarded with the most vivid abuse.

This intense love for, and faculty of perceiving, what one may call the "concrete picturesque," accounts for his many hard sayings about fiction and poetry. He could not understand people being at the trouble of inventing characters and situations when history was full of men and women; when streets were crowded and continents were being peopled under their very noses. Emerson's sphynx-like utterances irritated him at times, as they well might; his orations and the like. "I

long," he says, " to see some *concrete thing*, some
Event—Man's Life, American Forest, or piece of
Creation which this Emerson loves and wonders
at, well *Emersonised*, depicted by Emerson—filled
with the life of Emerson, and cast forth from him
then to live by itself." [1] But Carlyle forgot the
sluggishness of the ordinary imagination, and,
for the moment, the stupendous dullness of the
ordinary historian. It cannot be matter for
surprise that people prefer Smollett's *Humphrey
Clinker* to his *History of England*.

The third and last mark to which I call attention
is his humour. Nowhere, surely, in the whole field
of English literature, Shakespeare excepted, do
you come upon a more abundant vein of humour
than Carlyle's, though I admit that the quality
of the ore is not of the finest. His every production
is bathed in humour. This must never be, though
it often has been, forgotten. He is not to be taken
literally. He is always a humorist, not unfrequently
a writer of burlesque, and occasionally a buffoon.

[1] One need scarcely add, nothing of the sort ever proceeded from Emerson. How should it? Where was it to
come from? When, to employ language of Mr. Arnold's
own, "any poor child of nature" overhears the author of
Essays in Criticism telling two worlds that Emerson's
Essays are the most valuable prose contributions to the
literature of the century, his soul is indeed filled with "an
unutterable sense of lamentation and mourning and
woe." Mr. Arnold's silence was once felt to be provoking.
Wordsworth's lines kept occurring to one's mind—

> "Poor Matthew, all his frolics o'er,
>   Is silent as a standing pool."

But it was better so.

Although the spectacle of Mr. Swinburne taking Mr. Carlyle to task, as he recently did, for indelicacy, has an oddity all its own, so far as I am concerned I cannot but concur with this critic in thinking that Carlyle has laid himself open, particularly in his *Frederick the Great*, to the charge one usually associates with the great and terrible name of Dean Swift; but it is the Dean with a difference, and the difference is all in Carlyle's favour. The former deliberately pelts you with dirt, as did in old days gentlemen electors their parliamentary candidates; the latter only occasionally splashes you, as does a public vehicle pursuing on a wet day its uproarious course.

These, then, I take to be Carlyle's three principal marks or notes: mysticism in thought, realism in description, and humour in both.

To proceed now to his actual literary work.

First, then, I would record the fact that he was a great critic, and this at a time when our literary criticism was a scandal. He more than any other has purged our vision and widened our horizons in this great matter. He taught us there was no sort of finality, but only nonsense, in that kind of criticism which was content with laying down some foreign masterpiece with the observation that it was not suited for the English taste. He was, if not the first, almost the first critic, who pursued in his criticism the historical method, and sought to make us understand what we were required to judge. It has been said that Carlyle's criticisms are not final, and that he has not said the last word about Voltaire, Diderot, Richter, and Goethe. I can well believe it. But reserving "last words" for the use of the last man (to whom they would appear to belong), it is surely something to have said the *first* sensible words uttered in English on these important subjects. We ought not to forget the early days of the *Foreign* and *Quarterly Review*. We have critics now, quieter, more reposeful souls, taking their ease on Zion, who have entered upon a world ready to welcome them, whose keen rapiers may cut velvet better than did the two-handed broadsword of Carlyle, and whose later date may enable them to discern what their forerunner failed to perceive; but when the critics of this century come to be criticised by the critics of the next, an honourable, if not the highest place will be awarded to Carlyle.

Turn we now to the historian and biographer. History and biography much resemble one another in the pages of Carlyle, and occupy more than half his thirty-four volumes; nor is this to be wondered at, since they afforded him fullest scope for his three strong points—his love of the wonderful; his love of telling a story, as the children say, "from the very beginning"; and his humour. His view of history is sufficiently lofty. History, says he, is the true epic poem, a universal divine scripture whose plenary inspiration no one out of Bedlam shall bring into question. Nor is he quite at one with the ordinary historian as to the true historical method. "The time seems coming when he who sees no world but that of courts and camps, and writes only how soldiers were drilled and shot, and how this ministerial conjurer outconjured that other, and then guided, or at least held, something which he called the rudder of Government, but which was rather the spigot of Taxation, wherewith in place of steering he could tax, will pass for a more or less instructive Gazetteer, but will no longer be called an Historian."

Nor does the philosophical method of writing history please him any better:

"Truly if History is Philosophy teaching by examples, the writer fitted to compose history is hitherto an unknown man. Better were it that mere earthly historians should lower such pretensions, more suitable for omniscience than for human science, and aiming only at some picture of the things acted, which picture itself will be a poor approximation, leave the inscrutable purport of them an acknowledged secret—or at most, in reverent faith, pause over the mysterious vestiges of Him whose path is in the great deep of Time, whom History indeed reveals, but only all History and in Eternity will clearly reveal."

This same transcendental way of looking at things is very noticeable in the following view of Biography: "For, as the highest gospel was a Biography, so is the life of every good man still an indubitable gospel, and preaches to the eye and heart and whole man, so that devils even must believe and tremble, these gladdest tidings. Man is heaven-born—not the thrall of circumstances, of necessity, but the victorious subduer thereof." These, then, being his views, what are we to say of his works? His three principal historical works are, as every one knows, *Cromwell*, the *French Revolution*, and *Frederick the Great*, though there is a very considerable amount of other historical writing scattered up and down his works. But what are we to say of these three? Is he, by virtue of them, entitled to the rank and influence of a great historian? What have we a a right to demand of an historian? First, surely, stern veracity, which implies not merely knowledge but honesty. An historian stands in a fiduciary position towards his readers, and if he withholds from them important facts likely to influence their judgment, he is guilty of fraud, and, when justice is done in this world, will be condemned to refund all moneys he has made by his false professions, with compound interest. This sort of fraud is unknown to the law, but to nobody else. "Let me know the facts!" may well be the agonised cry of the student who finds himself floating down what Arnold has called "the vast Mississippi of falsehood, History." Secondly comes a catholic temper and way of looking at things. The historian should be a gentleman and possess a moral breadth of temperament. There should be no bitter protesting spirit about him. He should remember the world he has taken upon himself to write about is a large place, and that nobody set him up over us. Thirdly, he must be a born story-teller. If he is not this, he has mistaken his vocation. He may be a great philosopher, a useful editor, a profound scholar, and anything else his friends like to call him, except a great historian. How does Carlyle meet these requirements? His veracity, that is, his laborious accuracy, is admitted by the only persons competent to form an opinion, namely, independent investigators who have followed in his track; but what may be called the internal evidence of the case also supplies a strong proof of it. Carlyle was, as every one knows, a hero-worshipper. It is part of his mysticism. With him man, as well as God, is a spirit, either of good or evil, and as such should be either worshipped or reviled. He is never himself till he has discovered or invented a hero; and, when he has got him, he tosses and dandles him as a mother her babe. This is a terrible temptation to put in the way of an historian, and few there be who are found able to resist it. How easy to keep back an ugly fact, sure to be a stumbling-block in the way of weak brethren! Carlyle is above suspicion in this respect. He knows no reticence. Nothing restrains him; not even the so-called proprieties of history. He may, after his boisterous fashion, pour scorn upon you for looking grave, as you read in his vivid pages of the reckless manner in which too many of his heroes drove coaches-and-six through the Ten Commandments.

As likely as not he will call you a blockhead, and tell you to close your wide mouth and cease shrieking. But, dear me! hard words break no bones, and it is an amazing comfort to know the facts. Is he writing of Cromwell?—down goes everything—letters, speeches, as they were written, as they were delivered. Few great men are edited after this fashion. Were they to be so—Luther, for example—many eyes would be opened very wide. Nor does Carlyle fail in comment. If the Protector makes a somewhat distant allusion to the Barbadoes, Carlyle is at your elbow to tell you it means his selling people to work as slaves in the West Indies. As for Mirabeau, "our wild Gabriel Honoré," well! we are told all about him; nor is Frederick let off a single absurdity or atrocity. But when we have admitted the veracity, what are we to say of the catholic temper, the breadth of temperament, the wide Shakespearean tolerance? Carlyle ought to have them all. By nature he was tolerant enough; so true a humorist could never be a bigot. When his war-paint is not on, a child might lead him. His judgments are gracious, chivalrous, tinged with a kindly melancholy and divine pity. But this mood is never for long. Some gadfly stings him: he seizes his tomahawk and is off on the trail. It must sorrowfully be admitted that a long life of opposition and indigestion, of fierce warfare with cooks and Philistines, spoilt his temper, never of the best, and made him too often contemptuous, savage, unjust.

His language then becomes unreasonable, unbearable, bad. Literature takes care of herself. You disobey her rules: well and good, she shuts her door in your face; you plead your genius: she replies, "Your temper," and bolts it. Carlyle has deliberately destroyed, by his own wilfulness, the value of a great deal he has written. It can never become classical. Alas! that this should be true of too many eminent Englishmen of our time. Language such as was, at one time, almost habitual with Mr. Ruskin, is a national humiliation, giving point to the Frenchman's sneer as to our distinguishing literary characteristic being "*la brutalité*." In Carlyle's case much must be allowed for his rhetoric and humour. In slang phrase, he always "piles it on." Does a bookseller misdirect a parcel, he exclaims, "My malison on all Blockheadisms and Torpid Infidelities of which this world is full." Still, all allowances made, it is a thousand pities; and one's thoughts turn away from this stormy old man and take refuge in the quiet haven of the Oratory at Birmingham, with its great Protagonist, who, throughout an equally long life spent in painful controversy, and wielding weapons as terrible as Carlyle's own, has rarely forgotten to be urbane, and whose every sentence is a "thing of beauty." It must, then, be owned that too many of Carlyle's literary achievements "lack a gracious somewhat." By force of his genius he "smites the rock and spreads the water"; but then, like Moses, "he desecrates, belike, the deed in doing."

Our third requirement was, it may be remembered, the gift of the story-teller. Here one is on firm ground. Where is the equal of the man who has told us the story of *The Diamond Necklace*?

It is the vogue, nowadays, to sneer at picturesque writing. Professor Seeley, for reasons of his own, appears to think that whilst politics, and, I presume, religion, may be made as interesting as you please, history should be as dull as possible. This, surely, is a jaundiced view. If there is one thing it is legitimate to make more interesting than another, it is the varied record of man's life upon earth. So long as we have human hearts and await human destinies, so long as we are alive to the pathos, the dignity, the comedy of human life, so long shall we continue to rank above the philosopher, higher than the politician, the great artist, be he called dramatist or historian, who makes us conscious of the divine movement of events, and of our fathers who were before us. Of course we assume accuracy and labour in our animated historian; though, for that matter, other things being equal, I prefer a lively liar to a dull one.

Carlyle is sometimes as irresistible as " The Campbells are Coming," or " Auld Lang Syne." He has described some men and some events once and for all, and so takes his place with Thucydides, Tacitus and Gibbon. Pedants may try hard to forget this, and may in their laboured nothings seek to ignore the author of *Cromwell* and [the *French Revolution*; but as well might the pedes-

trian in Cumberland or Inverness seek to ignore
Helvellyn or Ben Nevis. Carlyle is *there*, and will
remain there, when the pedant of to-day has
been superseded by the pedant of to-morrow.

Remembering all this, we are apt to forget his
faults, his eccentricities and vagaries, his buffoon-
eries, his too-outrageous cynicisms and his too-
intrusive egotisms, and to ask ourselves—if it be
not this man, who is it then to be? Macaulay,
answer some; and Macaulay's claims are not of
the sort to go unrecognised in a world which loves
clearness of expression and of view only too well.
Macaulay's position never admitted of doubt. We
know what to expect, and we always get it. It is
like the old days of W. G. Grace's cricket. We
went to see the leviathan slog for six, and we saw
it. We expected him to do it, and he did it. So
with Macaulay—the good Whig, as he takes up
the *History*, settles himself down in his chair, and
knows it is going to be a bad time for the Tories.
Macaulay's style—his much-praised style—is in-
effectual for the purpose of telling the truth about
anything. It is splendid, but *splendide mendax*,
and in Macaulay's case the style was the man. He
had enormous knowledge, and a noble spirit; his
knowledge enriched his style and his spirit consecrated it to the service of Liberty. We do well
to be proud of Macaulay; but we must add that,
great as was his knowledge, great also was his
ignorance, which was none the less ignorance
because it was wilful; noble as was his spirit, the

range of subject over which it energised was painfully restricted. He looked out upon the world,
but, behold, only the Whigs were good. Luther
and Loyola, Cromwell and Claverhouse, Carlyle
and Newman—they moved him not; their en-
thusiasms were delusions, and their politics demonstrable errors. Whereas, of Lord Somers and
Charles first Earl Grey it is impossible to speak
without emotion. But the world does not belong
to the Whigs; and a great historian must be
capable of sympathising both with delusions and
demonstrable errors. Mr. Gladstone has com-
mented with force upon what he calls Macaulay's
invincible ignorance, and further says that to
certain aspects of a case (particularly those aspects
most pleasing to Mr. Gladstone), Macaulay's mind
was hermetically sealed. It is difficult to resist
these conclusions; and it would appear no rash
inference from them, that a man in a state of
invincible ignorance and with a mind hermetically
sealed, whatever else he may be—orator, advocate,
statesman, journalist, man of letters—can never
be a great historian. But, indeed, when one
remembers Macaulay's limited range of ideas; the
commonplaceness of his morality, and of his
descriptions; his absence of humour, and of
pathos—for though Miss Martineau says she found
one pathetic passage in the *History*, I have often
searched for it in vain; and then turns to Carlyle
—to his almost bewildering affluence of thought,
fancy, feeling, humour, pathos—his biting pen,

his scorching criticism, his world-wide sympathy (save in certain moods) with everything but the smug commonplace—to prefer Macaulay to him, is like giving the preference to Birket Foster over Salvator Rosa. But if it is not Macaulay, who is it to be? Mr. Hepworth Dixon or Mr. Froude? Of Bishop Stubbs and Professor Freeman it behoves every ignoramus to speak with respect. Horny-handed sons of toil, they are worthy of their wage. Carlyle has somewhere struck a distinction between the historical artist and the historical artisan. The bishop and the professor are historical artisans; artists they are not—and the great historian is a great artist.

England boasts two such artists. Edward Gibbon and Thomas Carlyle. The elder historian may be compared to one of the great Alpine roadways—sublime in its conception, heroic in its execution, superb in its magnificent uniformity of good workmanship. The younger resembles one of his native streams, pent in at times between huge rocks, and tormented into foam, and then effecting its escape down some precipice, and spreading into cool expanses below; but however varied may be its fortunes—however startling its changes—always in motion, always in harmony with the scene around. It is gloomy? It is with the gloom of the thunder-cloud. Is it bright? It is with the radiance of the sun.

It is with some consternation that I approach the subject of Carlyle's politics. One handles them as does an inspector of police a parcel reported to contain dynamite. The *Latter-Day Pamphlets* might not unfitly be labelled " Dangerous Explosives."

In this matter of politics there were two Carlyles; and, as generally happens in such cases, his last state was worse than his first. Up to 1843, he not unfairly might be called a Liberal—of uncertain vote it may be—a man difficult to work with, and impatient of discipline, but still aglow with generous heat; full of large-hearted sympathy with the poor and oppressed, and of intense hatred of the cruel and shallow sophistries that then passed for maxims, almost for axioms, of government. In the year 1819, when the yeomanry round Glasgow was called out to keep down some dreadful monsters called " Radicals," Carlyle describes how he met an advocate of his acquaintance hurrying along, musket in hand, to his drill on the Links. " You should have the like of this," said he, cheerfully patting his gun. " Yes," was the reply, " but I haven't yet quite settled on which side." And when he did make his choice, on the whole he chose rightly. The author of that noble pamphlet *Chartism*, published in 1840, was at least once a Liberal. Let me quote a passage that has stirred to effort many a generous heart now cold in death:

" Who would suppose that Education were a thing which had to be advocated on the ground of local expediency, or indeed on any ground? As if it stood not on the basis of an everlasting duty, as a prime necessity of man! It is a thing that should need no advocating; much as it does actually need. To impart the gift of thinking to those who cannot think, and yet who could in that case think: this, one would imagine, was the first function a government had to set about discharging. Were it not a cruel thing to see, in any province of an empire, the inhabitants living all mutilated in their limbs, each strong man with his right arm lamed? How much crueller to find the strong soul with its eyes still sealed— its eyes extinct, so that it sees not! Light has come into the world; but to this poor peasant it has come in vain. For six thousand years the sons of Adam, in sleepless effort, have been devising, doing, discovering; in mysterious, infinite, indissoluble communion, warring, a little band of brothers, against the black empire of necessity and night; they have accomplished such a conquest and conquests; and to this man it is all as if it had not been. The four-and-twenty letters of the alphabet are still runic enigmas to him. He passes by on the other side; and that great spiritual kingdom, the toil-won conquest of his own brothers, all that his brothers have conquered, is a thing not extant for him. An invisible empire; he knows it not—suspects it not. And is not this his withal; the conquest of his own brothers, the lawfully acquired possession of all men? Baleful enchantment lies over him, from generation to generation; he knows not that such an empire is his—that such an empire is his at all. . . . Heavier wrong is not done under the sun. It lasts from year to year, from century to century; the blinded sire slaves himself out, and leaves a blinded son; and men, made in the image of God, continue as two-legged beasts of labour: and in the largest empire of the world it is a debate whether a small fraction of the revenue of one day shall, after thirteen centuries, be laid out on it, or not laid out on it. Have we governors? Have we teachers? Have we had a Church these thirteen hundred years? What is an overseer of souls, an archoverseer, archiepiscopus? Is he something? If so, let him lay his hand on his heart and say what thing!"

Nor was the man who in 1843 wrote as follows altogether at sea in politics:

"Of Time Bill, Factory Bill, and other such Bills, the present editor has no authority to speak. He knows not, it is for others than he to know, in what specific ways it may be feasible to interfere with legislation between the workers and the master-workers—knows only and sees that legislative interference, and interferences not a few, are indispensable. Nay, interference has begun; there are already factory inspectors. Perhaps there might be mine inspectors too. Might there not be furrow-field inspectors withal, to ascertain how, on 7s. 6d. a week, a human family does live? Again, are not sanitary regulations possible for a legislature? Baths, free air, a wholesome temperature, ceilings twenty feet high, might be

ordained by Act of Parliament in all establish-
ments licensed as mills. There are such mills
already extant—honour to the builders of them.
The legislature can say to others, ' Go you and do
likewise—better if you can.' "

By no means a bad programme for 1843; and
a good part of it has been carried out, but with
next to no aid from Carlyle.

The Radical party has struggled on as best it
might, without the author of *Chartism* and the
French Revolution:

They have marched prospering, not through his presence;

and it is no party spirit that leads one to regret
the change of mind which prevented the later
public life of this great man, and now the memory
of it, from being enriched with something better
than a five-pound note for Governor Eyre.

But it could not be helped. What brought about
the rupture was his losing faith in the ultimate
destiny of man upon earth. No more terrible loss
can be sustained. It is of both heart and hope.
He fell back upon heated visions of heaven-sent
heroes, devoting their early days for the most
part to hoodwinking the people, and their latter
ones, more heroically, to shooting them.

But it is foolish to quarrel with results, and we
may learn something even from the later Carlyle.
We lay down John Bright's *Reform Speeches,* and
take up Carlyle and light upon a passage like this:
" Inexpressibly delirious seems to me the puddle

of Parliament and public upon what it calls the Reform Measure, that is to say, the calling in of new supplies of blockheadism, gullibility, bribability, amenability to beer and balderdash, by way of amending the woes we have had from previous supplies of that bad article." This view must be accounted for as well as Mr. Bright's. We shall do well to remember, with Carlyle, that the best of all Reform Bills is that which each citizen passes in his own breast, where it is pretty sure to meet with strenuous opposition. The reform of ourselves is no doubt an heroic measure never to be overlooked, and, in the face of accusations of gullibility, bribability, amenability to beer and balderdash, our poor humanity can only stand abashed, and feebly demur to the bad English in which the charges are conveyed. But we can't all lose hope. We remember Sir David Ramsay's reply to Lord Rea, once quoted by Carlyle himself. Then said his lordship: " Well, God mend all." " Nay, by God, Donald, we must help Him to mend it!" It is idle to stand gaping at the heavens, waiting to feel the thong of some hero of questionable morals and robust conscience; and therefore, unless Reform Bills can be shown to have checked purity of election, to have increased the stupidity of electors, and generally to have promoted corruption—which notoriously they have not—we may allow Carlyle to make his exit " swearing," and regard their presence in the Statute Book, if not with rapture, at least with equanimity.

But it must not be forgotten that the battle is still raging—the issue is still uncertain. Mr. Froude is still free to assert that the *post-mortem* will prove Carlyle was right. His political sagacity no reader of *Frederick* can deny; his insight into hidden causes and far-away effects was keen beyond precedent—nothing he ever said deserves contempt, though it may merit anger. If we would escape his conclusion, we must not altogether disregard his premises. Bankruptcy and death are the final heirs of imposture and make-believes. The old faiths and forms are worn too threadbare by a thousand disputations to bear the burden of the new democracy, which, if it is not merely to win the battle but to hold the country, must be ready with new faiths and forms of her own. They are within her reach if she but knew it; they lie to her hand: surely they will not escape her grasp! If they do not, then, in the glad day when worship is once more restored to man, he will with becoming generosity forget much that Carlyle has written, and remembering more, rank him amongst the prophets of humanity.

Carlyle's poetry can only be exhibited in long extracts, which would be here out of place, and might excite controversy as to the meaning of words, and draw down upon me the measureless malice of the metricists. There are, however, passages in *Sartor Resartus* and the *French Revolution* which have long appeared to me to be the sublimest poetry of the century; and it was therefore with great pleasure that I found Mr. Justice Stephen, in his book on *Liberty, Equality, and Fraternity,* introducing a quotation from the eighth chapter of the third book of *Sartor Resartus,* with the remark that " it is perhaps the most memorable utterance of the greatest poet of the age."

As for Carlyle's religion, it may be said he had none, inasmuch as he expounded no creed and put his name to no confession. This is the pedantry of the schools. He taught us religion, as cold water and fresh air teach us health, by rendering the conditions of disease well-nigh impossible. For more than half a century, with superhuman energy, he struggled to establish the basis of all religions, " reverence and godly fear." " Love not pleasure, love God; this is the everlasting Yea."

One's remarks might here naturally come to an end, with a word or two of hearty praise of the brave course of life led by the man who awhile back stood the acknowledged head of English letters. But the present time is not the happiest for a panegyric on Carlyle. It would be in vain to deny that the brightness of his reputation underwent an eclipse, visible everywhere, by the publication of his *Reminiscences.* They surprised most of us, pained not a few, and hugely delighted that ghastly crew, the wreckers of humanity, who are never so happy as when employed in pulling down great reputations to their own miserable levels. When these " baleful creatures," as Carlyle would have called them, have lit upon any passage indicative of conceit or jealousy or spite, they have fastened upon it and screamed over it, with a pleasure but ill-concealed and with a horror but ill-feigned. "Behold," they exclaim, "your hero robbed of the nimbus his inflated style cast around him—this preacher and fault-finder reduced to his principal parts: and lo! the main ingredient is most unmistakably ' bile '! "

The critic, however, has nought to do either with the sighs of the sorrowful, "mourning when a hero falls," or with the scorn of the malicious, rejoicing, as did Bunyan's Juryman, Mr. Live-loose, when Faithful was condemned to die: "I could never endure him, for he would always be condemning my way."

The critic's task is to consider the book itself, *i.e.*, the nature of its contents, and how it came to be written at all.

When this has been done, there will not be found much demanding moral censure; whilst the reader will note with delight, applied to the trifling concerns of life, those extraordinary gifts of observation and apprehension which have so often charmed him in the pages of history and biography.

These peccant volumes contain but four sketches: one of his father, written in 1832; the other three, of Edward Irving, Lord Jeffrey, and Mrs. Carlyle, all written after the death of the last-named, in 1866.

The only fault that has been found with the

27

first sketch is, that in it Carlyle hazards the assertion that Scotland does not now contain his
father's like. It ought surely to be possible to
dispute this opinion without exhibiting emotion.
To think well of their forebears is one of the few
weaknesses of Scotchmen. This sketch, as a whole,
must be carried to Carlyle's credit, and is a per-
manent addition to literature. It is pious, after
the high Roman fashion. It satisfies our finest
sense of the fit and proper. Just exactly so should
a literate son write of an illiterate peasant father.
How immeasurable seems the distance between
the man from whom proceeded the thirty-four
volumes we have been writing about and the
Calvinistic mason who didn't even know his Burns!
—and yet here we find the whole distance spanned
by filial love.

The sketch of Lord Jeffrey is inimitable. One
was getting tired of Jeffrey, and prepared to give
him the go-by, when Carlyle creates him afresh,
and, for the first time, we see the bright little man
bewitching us by what he is, disappointing us
by what he is not. The spiteful remarks the
sketch contains may be considered, along with
those of the same nature to be found only too
plentifully in the remaining two papers.

After careful consideration of the worst of these
remarks, Mrs. Oliphant's explanation seems the
true one; they are most of them sparkling bits
of Mrs. Carlyle's conversation. She, happily for
herself, had a lively wit, and, perhaps not so

happily, a biting tongue, and was, as Carlyle tells us, accustomed to make him laugh, as they drove home together from London crushes, by far from genial observations on her fellow-creatures, little recking—how should she?—that what was so lightly uttered was being engraven on the tablets of the most marvellous of memories, and was destined long afterwards to be written down in grim earnest by a half-frenzied old man, and printed, in cold blood, by an English gentleman.

The horrible description of Mrs. Irving's personal appearance, and other stories in the same connexion, are recognised by Mrs. Oliphant as in substance Mrs. Carlyle's; whilst the malicious account of Mrs. Basil Montague's head-dress is attributed by Carlyle himself to his wife. Still, after dividing the total, there is a good helping for each, and blame would justly be Carlyle's due if we did not remember, as we are bound to do, that, interesting as these three sketches are, their interest is pathological, and ought never to have been given us. Mr. Froude should have read them in tears, and burnt them in fire. There is nothing surprising in the state of mind which produced them. They are easily accounted for by our sorrow-laden experience. It is a familiar feeling which prompts a man, suddenly bereft of one whom he alone really knew and loved, to turn in his fierce indignation upon the world and deride its idols whom all are praising, and which yet to him seem ugly by the side of one of whom no one speaks. To be angry with such a sentence as " scribbling Sands and Eliots, not fit to compare with my incomparable Jeannie," is at once inhuman and ridiculous. This is the language of the heart, not of the head. It is no more criticism than is the trumpeting of a wounded elephant zoology.

Happy is the man who at such a time holds both peace and pen; but unhappiest of all is he who, having dipped his sorrow into ink, entrusts the manuscript to a romantic historian.

The two volumes of the *Life* and the three volumes of Mrs. Carlyle's *Correspondence* unfortunately did not pour oil upon the troubled waters. The partisanship they evoked was positively indecent. Mrs. Carlyle had her troubles and her sorrows, as have most women who live under the same roof with a man of creative genius; but of one thing we may be quite sure, that she would have been the first, to use her own expressive language, to require God " particularly to damn " her impertinent sympathisers. As for Mr. Froude, he may yet discover his Nemesis in the spirit of an angry woman whose privacy he has invaded, and whose diary he has most wantonly published.

These dark clouds are ephemeral. They will roll away, and we shall once more gladly recognise the lineaments of an essentially lofty character, of one who, though a man of genius and of letters, neither outraged society nor stooped to it; was neither a rebel nor a slave; who in poverty scorned wealth; who never mistook popularity for fame; but from the first assumed, and throughout maintained, the proud attitude of one whose duty it was to teach and not to tickle mankind.

Brother-dunces, lend me your ears! not to crop, but that I may whisper into their furry depths: "Do not quarrel with genius. We have none ourselves, and yet are so constituted that we cannot live without it."

GAY'S FABLES

By Austin Dobson

No material addition, in the way of supplementary
information, can now be made to the frequently
reprinted "Life of Gay" in Johnson's *Poets* or to
the genial and kindly sketch in Thackeray's
English Humourists. Still, in a consideration of his
Fables, some brief account of him may fairly be
expected. He was born in 1688 at Barnstaple in
Devonshire. He came of an old but impoverished
family, and was educated under a local school-
master of certain pretensions to literature, who is
affirmed to have been the author of a volume of
Latin and English verses. Johnson says this
worthy's name was Luck. If so, he must have
been the "R. Luck, A.M., Master of Barnstaple
School," whose poems were published by Cave
in April 1736; but it is most likely that Gay's
earliest preceptor was a predecessor of Luck's,
whom Pope called William Rayner, and who was
also accused of versifying. Whatever progress
the future fabulist made under these instructors,
it is clear from his subsequent career that he had
more than a bowing acquaintance with the classics.
Indeed, there is still preserved in the " Forster

Library " at South Kensington, a large-paper copy of Mattaire's *Horace* (Tonson and Watts, 1715), which contains Gay's autograph, and is copiously annotated in his beautiful handwriting. This of itself should be sufficient to refute the aspersions cast upon his scholarship by a recent critic of Swift; for it affords certain evidence that even at twenty-seven, and perhaps at a much later period, he was a diligent student of the charming lyrist and satirist who, above all others, commends himself to the attention of idle men. In his boyhood, however, it must be assumed that Gay's indolence was more strongly developed than his application, for his friends could find no better opening for him than that of apprentice to a London silk-mercer. With this vocation he was speedily dissatisfied. The late John Hill Burton, in his *History of the Reign of Queen Anne*, implies that he ran away; but there is nothing to show that he took any step of so energetic a character. The most reasonable supposition is, that after spending some time idly in his native place, he returned to London to try his fortune with letters. At that time the swarming clubs and coffee-houses afforded opportunities of access to literary notabilities, now scarcely conceivable; and Gay was of a temper to find friends. Of his earliest efforts no record has been preserved. Gossipers, it is said, asserted in after days that he was employed for some time as amanuensis to Aaron Hill, notorious subsequently for that quarrel with Pope which won him the honours of

33

the *Dunciad*. But to 1708—on Hill's authority
—is assigned Gay's first published poem, *Wine*,
the purport of which may be gathered from the—

Nulla placere diu, nec vivere carmina possunt,
Quæ scribuntur aquæ potoribus—

of its motto, a disputed theory which seems to
have " exercised " the author nearly all his life.
He claims, in this production, to " draw Miltonic
air "; but the atmosphere is more suggestive of
the *Splendid Shilling* than of *Paradise Lost*, a fact
which may account for the omission of the verses
from the later quarto of 1720. In 1712 he contributed a translation of one of Ovid's *Metamor-
phoses* to the famous " Rape of the Lock " volume
of Lintot's *Miscellaneous Poems and Translations*,
and in the same year he became " secretary or
domestic steward " to the Duchess of Monmouth
—that " virtuous and excellent lady," as Evelyn
calls her—whose husband had been beheaded in
1685. It was probably in this capacity that he
made the acquaintance of Pope, who was his own
age, and to whom, in 1713, he dedicated his *Rural
Sports, a Georgic*, which displays a good deal of
unconventional knowledge of country-life, and
especially of hunting and fishing. This characteristic no doubt induced Pope to invoke his aid
in the crusade he was then waging against the
artificial pastoral of Ambrose Phillips; and Gay's
Shepherd's Week, 1714, was the result of this
alliance. He was to depict rusticity after " the
true ancient guise of Theocritus," or, in plainer

words, by representing it in its blowsed and unkempt reality, to cast merited ridicule upon the "mild Arcadians" of the period. But the humour and keen observation of his pictures attracted more attention than their satirical purpose; and they may still be studied with pleasure for their folk-lore and their homely fidelity to nature. From a biographical point of view, however, the most interesting part of the *Shepherd's Week* is its prologue to Bolingbroke, the allusions in which seem to show that the some-time mercer's apprentice had already made the acquaintance of Arbuthnot, and probably of some fairer critics whose favour was of greater importance to poetical advancement. "No more"—he says—

> No more I'll sing *Buxoma* brown,
> Like goldfinch in her *Sunday* gown;
> Nor *Clumsilis*, nor *Marian* bright,
> Nor damsel that *Hobnelia* hight.
> But *Lansdown* fresh as flow'r of *May*,
> And *Berkely* lady blithe and gay,
> And *Anglesey*, whose speech exceeds
> The voice of pipe, or oaten reeds;
> And blooming *Hyde*, with eyes so rare,
> And *Montague* beyond compare.

"Blooming *Hyde*, with eyes so rare," was Lady Jane Hyde, daughter of the Earl of Rochester, and elder sister of the "Kitty, beautiful and young," who was subsequently to be Gay's warmest friend. Early in the year in which the *Shepherd's Week* appeared, Gay, who—as he says—was now "quite off" with the Duchess of Monmouth, obtained the appointment, by Swift's interest, of Secretary to Lord Clarendon (Lord Rochester's cousin), then Envoy-Extraordinary to the Court of Hanover; and there exists a curious rhymed petition from the needy poet to Lord Treasurer Oxford, in which he solicits funds to enable him to set out on his journey. For a brief space we must imagine him strutting " in silver and blue " through the clipped avenues of Herrenhausen, yawning over the routine life of the little German court, and perfecting himself in the diplomatic arts of " bowing profoundly, speaking deliberately, and wearing both sides of his long periwig before." Then the death of Queen Anne put an end to these halcyon days. What was worse, the *Shepherd's Week* had been dedicated to Bolingbroke; and Bolingbroke, as ill-luck would have it, was not in favour with Her Majesty's successor. In this strait, as a course which " could do no harm," Pope counselled his hapless friend to " write something on the King, or Prince, or Princess." Thereupon Gay prepared an *Epistle to a Lady, occasion'd by the Arrival of Her Royal Highness* (*i.e.* the Princess of Wales), in which he touches plaintively upon the forlorn hopes of impecunious suitors:

> Pensive each night, from room to room I walk'd,
> To one I bow'd, and with another talk'd;
> Enquir'd what news, or such a Lady's name,
> And did the next day, and the next, the same.
> Places, I found, were daily giv'n away,
> And yet no friendly Gazette mentioned *Gay*.

The only appreciable result of this ingenuous appeal would seem to have been that the Prince and Princess of Wales came to see the " tragi-comi-pastoral farce " of the *What d'ye call it*, which Gay produced in 1715, and of which the sole enduring part is the musical ballad, " 'Twas when the seas were roaring." In the following year he published *Trivia ; or, The Art of Walking the Streets of London*," in three books, an unexpected theme for an author whose tastes were certainly not pedestrian. In the " Advertisement " to this, he acknowledges the aid of Swift; and it is, indeed, not improbable that *Trivia* was originally suggested by the *Morning* and *City Shower* which Swift had previously contributed to the *Tatler*. However this may be, Gay's poem is sprightly and readable, and full of interest for the antiquary and student of eighteenth-century " humours." The coarse and ill-advised comedy of *Three Hours after Marriage*, which he wrote with Pope and Arbuthnot, and of which he bore the failure, may be passed over without further mention. During all this period he seems to have been vaguely expecting court favour, and to have suffered most of the discouragements of hope deferred. Yet if the court neglected his pretensions,—and it nowhere appears that they were very urgent or very valid,—he found friends whose kindness took a practical form. In 1716, Lord Burlington sent him into Devonshire; in the year following, Pulteney, afterwards Earl of Bath, carried him to Aix, and in 1718 he went with Lord Harcourt to Oxfordshire, where befell that pretty tragedy of the two haymakers struck by lightning, which sentimental Mr. Pope made the subject of a famous letter to Lady Mary Wortley Montagu, who, unluckily for sentiment, received it in anything but a sympathetic spirit. The journeys to Exeter and Aix were commemorated in a couple of epistles, not more spontaneous than most tributary verse. These, with other pieces, ultimately found a place in the fine quarto edition of Gay's poems which Tonson and Lintot published in 1720, with a frontispiece by the eminent William Kent, and a list of subscribers rivalling in number, and exceeding in interest, that prefixed to the *Prior* of 1718. Those munificent patrons of literature, the Earl of Burlington and the Duke of Chandos, took fifty copies apiece. Truly the poet was right when, in a more sanguine moment, he wrote that " he knew no age so justly to be instiled *Golden* " as that in which he lived!

Among the other names on the subscription-list are two which have an especial attraction in Gay's life, for they are those of his kindest and most attached friends, the Duke and Duchess of Queensberry. The lady was the charming and wayward Catharine Hyde,—the " Kitty " whose first appearance at Drury Lane play-house as a triumphant beauty of eighteen, Prior had celebrated in some of his brightest and airiest verses, and whose picture, as a milkmaid of quality, painted by

Jervas at a later date, is to be seen in the " National Portrait Gallery." As already stated, Gay had written of her sister Jane (by this time Countess of Essex) as far back as 1714; and it may be that her own acquaintance with him dated from the same period. But after her marriage to the Duke of Queensberry in 1720, she appears to have taken him completely under her protection. " He [Gay] is always with the Duchess of Queensberry," writes Mrs. Bradshaw to Mrs. Howard in 1721; and, in 1726, the poet himself tells Swift that he has been with his patrons at Oxford and at Petersham, and "wheresoever they would carry me." In the intervals he is helping Congreve to nurse his gout " at the *Bath*," or " living almost altogether " with Lord Burlington at Chiswick, or acting as amanuensis to Pope (" which, you know, is no idle charge "), or borrowing sheets from Jervas to entertain Swift in those lodgings at Whitehall which had been granted to him by the Earl of Lincoln, and which were taken from him by Sir Robert Walpole. It speaks much for the charm of his character that he knew how to acquire and to retain friends so constant and so diverse. But the baseless hopes that haunt the unenergetic seem never to have deserted him. At one time he was supposed to have been the possessor of an ample fortune in South Sea stock, which vanished while he was deciding what to do with it; and again he looked confidently for advancement to the accession of the Prince and

Princess of Wales. His hopes were dashed to the ground by a nomination as Gentleman Usher to the little Princess Louisa, a post for which he rightly thought himself too old. Yet he was never without some compensations. By the *quarto* edition of his *Poems* he made £1000, and he was to be more fortunate still.

Since 1720 he had written but little of importance. The tragedy of the *Captives*, which appeared in 1724, had small success on the stage, and in 1727 he published the first series of the *Fables*, to which fuller reference will be made hereafter. But on the 29th of January 1728 was produced, at Lincoln's Inn Fields, his famous *Beggar's Opera*, which for a season overthrew Italian song—" that Dagon of the Nobility and Gentry, who had so long seduced them to idolatry," as the *Companion to the Playhouse* puts it—and made its author's name a household word. How it first occurred to Swift what " an odd pretty sort of thing a Newgate Pastoral might make "; how friends hesitated, and Cibber rejected, and the public rapturously applauded; how it was sung at street-corners and painted on screens; how it procured its " Polly " a coronet; and made Rich [the manager] gay, and Gay [the author] rich—all these things are the commonplaces of literature. At Mr. John Murray's in Albemarle Street may still be seen one of the pictures which William Hogarth painted of that all-conquering company, and which, years afterwards, was engraved by William Blake. The

Coryphæus of the highway (Walker) appears in the centre, while " Lucy " (Mrs Egleton) pleads for him to the left, and " Polly " (Miss Fenton) to the right. Rich, and the Duke of Bolton, who married Miss Fenton, are among the spectators. Scandal, in the person of John, Lord Hervey, adds that the opera owed a part of its popularity to something in the dilemma of Macheath, which irresistibly suggested the equally equivocal position of Walpole between his wife and his mistress. This is probably exaggerated; but it accounts in a measure for the fate which befell Gay's next enterprise.

That some attempt to perpetuate so splendid a success as the *Beggar's Opera* should not be made was scarcely in the nature of things; and Gay set speedily about the preparation of a sequel, to which he gave the name of the popular heroine of the earlier piece. But *Polly* was saved from the common fate of continuations by the action of the Lord Chamberlain, taken, it is supposed, upon the instruction of Walpole. When it was almost ready for rehearsal, the representation was prohibited. The result of this not very far-sighted step upon the part of the authorities was to surround its publication as a book (1729) with an unprecedented and wholly fictitious interest. Friends on all sides, and especially those opposed to the court, strained every nerve to promote the sale. The Duchess of Marlborough gave £100 for a copy; and the Duchess of Queensberry, who had the temerity to solicit subscriptions within the very precincts of St. James's, was forbidden to return to them. Thereupon the Duke, who was not on the best terms with the ministers, threw up his appointments, and followed his lady, who delivered a Parthian shaft in the shape of a very indiscreet and saucy letter to his Majesty King George. In all this it is plain that Gay's misfortune was simply made the instrument of political antagonisms; but, for the moment, his name was on every lip. " The inoffensive *John Gay* "—writes Arbuthnot to Swift under date of March 19, 1729—" is now become one of the obstructions to the peace of *Europe*, the terror of the ministers, the chief author of the *Craftsman* and all the seditious pamphlets which have been published against the Government. He has got several turned out of their places; the greatest ornament of the court banished from it for his sake; another great lady [Mrs. Howard, afterwards Countess of Suffolk] in danger of being *chassé* [*sic*] likewise; about seven or eight duchesses pushing forward, like the antient *circumcelliones* in the Church, who shall suffer martyrdom upon his account first. He is the darling of the city. . . . I can assure you, this is the very identical *John Gay* whom you formerly knew, and lodged with in *Whitehall* two years ago." The gross result was that Gay made about £1200 by the publication of *Polly*, of which Bowyer, the printer, struck off 10,500 copies in one year; by the representation of the *Beggar's Opera* he had

made, according to his own account, " between
£700 and £800."

During a great part of 1728 Gay resided at Bath
with the Duchess of Marlborough. After the pro-
hibition of *Polly*, he appears to have fallen ill, and
was tenderly nursed by Arbuthnot. Then the
Queensberrys took formal charge of him; and
henceforth he resided entirely either at their town-
house in Burlington Gardens, or at their country-
seat of Amesbury in Wiltshire. The Duke kept the
poet's money for him; the Duchess watched over
the poet himself. In the Swift correspondence
there are some charming joint letters to the Dean
in Ireland from Gay and his patroness, and they
give a most engaging picture of this alliance of
the fabulist and the *grande dame de par le monde*
of the last century. Walpole speaks of the latter
as her " mad grace "; and Mrs. Delany, who knew
her well, sighs piously over her long-protracted
eccentricities; but in this connexion she is altogether charming. As these letters have been
somewhat neglected by Gay's biographers, one of
them is reprinted here. It is by no means a pattern
" eighteenth-century epistle," not having been
composed (like Pope's and Walpole's) with an
eye to future publication; but it is thoroughly
characteristic of the writers, and is certainly not
wanting in some of that vivacity and cheerfulness
which (we are told) is seldom absent from the best
models. Amesbury, from which it is dated, now,
alas! no longer exists, and a summer-house is all

that remains of the buildings as they were in the time of Gay and his kind protectress.

Amesbury, Dec. the 6th, 1730.

DEAR SIR,

Both your letters, to my great satisfaction, I have received. You were mistaken as to my being in town; for I have been here ever since the beginning of *May*. But the best way is to direct your letters always to the duke's house, in *London*; and they are sent hither by his porter. You say, we deserve envy: I think, we do; for I envy no man, either in town or out of it. We have had some few visitors, and every one of them such, as one would desire to visit. The duchess is a more severe check upon my finances than ever you were; and I submit, as I did to you, to comply to my own good. I was a long time, before I could prevail with her to let me allow myself a pair of shoes with two heels; for I had lost one, and the shoes were so decayed, that they were not worth mending. You see by this, that those, who are the most generous of their own, can be the most covetous for others. I hope you will be so good to me, as to use your interest with her (for, whatever she says, you seem to have some) to indulge me with the extravagance suitable to my fortune.

The lady you mention, that dislikes you, hath no discernment. I really think, you may safely venture to *Amesbury*, though indeed the lady here likes to have her own way as well as you; which may sometimes occasion disputes: and, I tell you beforehand, that I cannot take your part. I think her so often in the right, that you will have great difficulty to persuade me that she is in the wrong. Then, there is another thing I ought to tell you, to deter you from this place; which is, that the lady of the house is not given to shew civility to those she does not like. She speaks her mind, and loves truth. For the uncommonness of the thing, I fancy, your curiosity will prevail over your fear; and you will like to see such a woman. But I say no more, till I know whether her grace will fill up the rest of the paper.

[*The Duchess continues.*]

Write I must, particularly now, as I have an opportunity to indulge my predominant passion of contradiction. I do, in the first place, contradict most things Mr. *Gay* says of me, to deter you from coming here; which, if you ever do, I hereby assure you, that, unless I like my own way better, you shall have yours, and in all disputes you shall convince me, if you can. But, by what I see of you, this is not a misfortune, that will always happen; for I find you are a great mistaker. For example, you take prudence for imperiousness: 'tis from this first, that I determined not to like one, who is too giddy-headed for me to be certain whether or no I shall ever be acquainted with. I have known people take great delight in building castles in the air; but I should choose to build friends upon a more solid foundation. I would fain know you; for I often hear more good likeable things than 'tis possible any one can deserve. Pray, come, that I may find out something wrong; for I, and I believe, most women, have an inconceivable pleasure to find out any faults, except their own. Mr. *Cibber* [1] is made poet laureat.

I am, Sir, as much your humble servant as I can be to any person I don't know.

C. Q.

Mr. *Gay* is very peevish that I spell and write ill: but I don't care: for neither the pen nor I can do better. Besides, I think you have flattered me, and such people ought to be put to trouble.

Other letters follow, most of them written from

---

[1] Harmonious *Cibber* entertains
The Court with annual Birth-day Strains;
Whence *Gay* was banish'd in Disgrace.
SWIFT, *On Poetry : a Rapsody*, 1733.

Amesbury, and bearing the same burden—the invitation of Swift to England. The last of the series is dated November 16, 1732; and in this Gay reports that he has come to London before the family, " to follow his own inventions," which included the production of his recently-written opera of *Achilles*. A few days later he was attacked by a constitutional malady to which he had long been subject, and died on the 4th of December. After lying in state in Exeter 'Change, he was (says Arbuthnot) " interred at *Westminster-Abbey*, as if he had been a peer of the realm," and the Queensberrys erected a handsome monument to his memory. By other friends he was mourned as sincerely, if not as sumptuously. Pope seems to have felt a genuine sorrow, and five days elapsed before Swift at Dublin could summon courage to open the letter which announced his death. His fortune, of which his patrons had made themselves the voluntary stewards, amounted to about £6000. It was divided between his sisters, Mrs. Baller and Mrs. Fortescue.

His last letter to Swift had ended thus : " Believe me, as I am, unchangeable in the regard, love and esteem I have for you." These words reveal the chief source of his personal charm. He was thoroughly kindly and affectionate, with just that touch of clinging in his nature, and of helplessness in his character, which, when it does not inspire contempt (and Gay's parts secured him from that), makes a man the spoiled child of men and the playfellow of women. He had his frailties, it is true; he was as indolent as Thomson; as fond of fine clothes as Goldsmith; as great a *gourmand* as La Fontaine. That he was also easily depressed and despondent was probably the result of his inactive life and his uncertain health. But, at his best, he must have been a delightfully equable and unobtrusive companion—invaluable for fêtes and gala-days, and equally well-adapted for the half-lights and unrestrained intercourse of familiar life. "You will never"—writes Swift to the Duchess of Queensberry—"be able to procure another so useful, so sincere, so virtuous, so disinterested, so entertaining, so easy, and so humble a friend, as that person whose death all good men lament." The praise is high, but there is little doubt that it was genuine. Pope's antithetical epitaph, despite the terrible mangling it has received at the hands of Johnson, may also be here quoted:

Of manners gentle, of affections mild;
In wit a man; simplicity, a child:
With native humour temp'ring virtuous rage,
Form'd to delight at once and lash the age:
Above temptation, in a low estate,
And uncorrupted, e'en among the great:
A safe companion, and an easy friend,
Unblamed through life, lamented in thy end.
These are thy honours! not that here thy bust
Is mix'd with heroes, or with kings thy dust,
But that the worthy and the good shall say,
Striking their pensive bosoms—*Here* lies GAY.

The monument in Westminster Abbey, for which

the above was composed, bears in addition a couplet of Gay's own:

> Life is a jest, and all things show it;
> I thought so once, but now I know it.

It is not necessary to attempt any detailed examination of Gay's works. Those among them most likely to attract the nineteenth-century reader have been mentioned in the course of the foregoing pages. Stripped of the adventitious circumstances which threw a halo of notoriety around them, his two best-known plays remain of interest chiefly for their songs, which have all the qualities songs possess when the writer, besides being a poet, is a musician as well. This lyric faculty is also present in all Gay's lesser pieces, and is as manifest in the ballad on pretty Miss Nelly Bennet at the French Court, as in " Black-Eyed Susan " or " 'Twas when the Seas were roaring." In his longer poems he seems always happiest when he is most unconstrained and natural, or treads the *terra firma* of the world he knows. The *Fan*, the *Eclogues*, the *Epistles*, are all more or less forced and conventional. But exceptions occur even in these. There is a foretaste of Fielding in the *Birth of the Squire*; and the *Welcome from Greece*, in which he congratulates Pope upon his successful translation of the *Iliad*, has a brightness of movement which seems to be the result of an unusually fresh inspiration. It is written, moreover, in an *ottava rima* stanza far earlier than Tennant's or Frere's or Byron's. The *Tales* are mediocre and generally

indelicate; the *Translations* have no special merit.
In the *Fables* he presented to his readers, Gay
found a more congenial vocation. The easy octo-
syllabic measure, not packed and idiomatic like
Swift's, not light and ironical like Prior's, but
ambling, colloquial, and even a little down-at-
heel, after the fashion of the bard himself, suited
his habits and his Muse. An uncompromising
criticism might perhaps be inclined to hint that
these little pieces are by no means faultless; that
they are occasionally deficient in narrative art,
that they lack real variety of theme, and that
they are often wearisome, almost unmanly, in
their querulous insistence on the vices of servility
and the hollowness of courts. On the other hand,
it must be admitted that they are full of *bonhomie*
and good sense; and if not characterised by the
highest philosophic wisdom, show much humorous
" criticism of life " and practical observation of
mankind. They have, too, some further recom-
mendations, which can scarcely be ignored. They
have given pleasure to several generations of
readers, old and young; and they have enriched
the language with more than one indispensable
quotation. " When a lady's in the case," and
" Two of a trade can ne'er agree," are still part
of the current coin of conversation.

THE POETRY OF EDGAR ALLAN POE

By Andrew Lang

THE life of Edgar Allan Poe, is, fortunately, a subject that but little concerns readers of his poetry. As far as the events of his career illustrate the enigmatic character of his genius, we have, perhaps, a right to inquire about them. We may imagine that from parents of semi-Celtic stock and artistic profession he inherited his genius, and that his pride and perversity came from his training by a wealthy injudicious foster-father. But the legend or myth of his errors and misfortunes, so often told and retold by posthumous malice or by too fond indulgence, is really no affair of ours. Poe's career is still a topic that excites controversy in America. The spite of his first biographer, Griswold, was begetting a natural reaction when Mr. Ingram published his *Edgar Allan Poe* (London, 1880), and unwittingly stirred up the hatred of surviving scandalmongers. Men are alive who knew Poe, and who suffered from his scornful criticism. To find their dead enemy defended by an Englishman excited their spleen, and, for other reasons, fairer American critics were not conciliated. The defence of this luckless man of genius is not, and cannot be, a wholly successful one. The viler charges and insinuations of Griswold may be refuted, but no skill can make Poe seem an amiable or an ascetic human being. It is natural that admirers of a poet's genius should wish to think well of the man, should wish to see him among the honourable, gentle, kindly, and wise. But Poe wanted as a man what his poetry also lacks; he wanted humanity. Among the passions, he was familiar with pride, and with the intolerable regret, the life-long *desiderium* which, having lost the solitary object of its love, can find among living men and women no more than the objects of passing sentiment and affectionate caprice. Love, as the poets have known it, from Catullus to Coventry Patmore, love, whether wild and feverish or stable and domestic, appears to have been to him unknown. And by this it is not meant that Poe was not an affectionate husband of his wife, but that the stronger part of his affections, the better element of his heart, had burned away before he was a man. He knew what he calls " that sorrow which the living love to cherish for the dead, and which, in some minds, resembles the delirium of opium." His spirit was always beating against the gate of the grave, and the chief praise he could confer on a woman in his maturity was to compare her to one whom he had lost while he was still a boy. " For months after her decease," says Mr. Ingram, " Poe . . . would go nightly to visit the tomb of his revered friend, and when the nights were very drear and cold, when the autumnal rains fell, and the winds wailed mournfully over the graves, he lingered longest and came away most regretfully."

The truth of this anecdote would be more important for our purpose than a world of controversies as to whether Poe was expelled from school, or gambled, or tippled, or why he gave up the editorship of this or that journal. We see him preoccupied, even in his boyhood, with the thought of death and of the condition of the dead. In his prose romances his imagination is always morbidly busy with the secrets of the sepulchre. His dead men speak, his corpses hold long colloquies with themselves, his characters are prematurely buried and explore the veiled things of corruption, his lovers are led wandering among the *hic jacets* of the dead. This is the dominant note of all his poetry, this wistful regret, almost hopeless of any reunion of departed souls in " the distant Aidenn," and almost fearful that the sleep of the dead is not dreamless.

> The lady sleeps! Oh may her sleep,
> Which is enduring, so be deep!

. . . .

> I pray to God that she may lie
> Forever with unopened eye,
> While the dim sheeted ghosts go by!

Thus Poe's verse is so far from being a " criticism

of life," that it is often, in literal earnest, a criticism of death; and even when his thoughts are not busy with death, even when his heart is not following some Lenore or Annabel Lee or Ulalume, his fancy does not deal with solid realities, with human passions. He dwells in a world more vaporous than that of Shelley's *Witch of Atlas*, in a region where dreaming cities crumble into fathomless seas, in a fairyland with "dim vales and shadowy woods," in haunted palaces, or in a lost and wandering star.

Not only was Poe's practice thus limited, but his theory of poetry was scarcely more extensive. He avowed that "melancholy is the most legitimate of all the poetical tones." This preference was, doubtless, caused by Poe's feeling that melancholy is the emotion most devoid of actual human stuff, the most etherealised, so to speak, the least likely to result in action. Poetry he defined as "the rhythmical creation of beauty," and beauty was in his eyes most beautiful when it was least alloyed with matter. Thus such topics as war, patriotism, prosperous love, religion, duty, were absolutely alien to the genius of Poe. He carried his theory to the absurd length of preferring Fouqué's *Undine* to the works of "fifty Molières." There is no poet more full of humanity than Molière, and no creature of fancy so empty as Undine, a sprite who is no more substantial than a morning shower, a vapour more evanescent than a solar myth. Poe, who liked the melancholy moods of this waste-watery sprite better than all the mirth and tenderness and passion of the Mascarilles and Alcestes, the Don Juans and Tartuffes, was also of opinion that no poem could be long. The *Iliad* and the *Odyssey*, he thought, were mistakes; they carried too heavy a weight of words and matter. When examined, this theory or paradox of Poe's shrinks into the commonplace observations that Poe preferred lyric poetry and that lyrics are essentially brief. In considering Poe's theory and practice, we must not forget that both were, in part, the result of reaction. American literature then intended to be extremely moral, and respectable, and didactic, and much of it was excessively uninspired. Poetry was expected, as she so often is expected, to teach morality as her main duty. We have always plenty of critics who cry out that poetry should be " palpitating with actuality," should struggle with " the living facts of the hour," should dignify industrialism, and indite pæans, perhaps, to sewing-machines and patent electric lights. Poe's nature was essentially rebellious, scornful, and aristocratic. If democratic ecstasies are a tissue of historical errors and self-complacent content with the commonplace, no one saw that more clearly than Poe. Thus he was the more encouraged by his rebellious instinct to take up what was then a singular and heterodox critical position. He has lately been called immoral in America for writing these words: " Beyond the limits of beauty the province of poetry does not extend. Its sole arbiter is taste. With the intellect or the conscience it has only collateral relations. It has no dependence, unless incidentally, upon either duty or truth."

To any one who believes that the best, the immortal poetry, is nobly busied with great actions and great passions, Poe's theory seems fatally narrow. Without the conceptions of duty and truth we can have no *Antigone* and no *Prometheus*. The great and paramount ideas have always been the inspirers of honourable actions, and by following them men and women are led into the dramatic situations which are the materials of Shakespeare, Æschylus, and Homer. There is an immortal strength in the stories of great actions; but Poe in theory and practice disdains all action and rejects this root of immortality. He deliberately discards *sanity*, he deliberately chooses *fantasy* for his portion. Now, while it is not the business of poetry to go about distributing tracts, she can never neglect actions and situations which, under her spell, become unconscious lessons of morality. But, as we have said, Poe's natural bent, and his reaction against the cheap didactic criticism of his country and his time, made him neglect all actions and most passions, both in his practice and his theory. When he spoke of Keats as the most flawless of English poets, and of Mr. Tennyson as " the noblest poet that ever lived," he was attracted by that in them which is most magical, most intangible, and most undefinable—the inimitable and inexpressible charm of their music, by the delicious languor of the *Ode to the Nightingale* and of the *Lotus-Eaters*. These poems are, indeed, examples of the " rhythmical creation of beauty," which, to Poe's mind, was the essence and function of poetry.

As to the nature of Poe's secret and the *technique* by which he produced his melodies, much may be attributed to the singular musical appropriateness of his words and epithets, much to his elaborate care for the details of his art. George Sand, in *Un Hiver à Majorque*, describes a rainy night which Chopin passed in the half-ruinous monastery where they lived. She tells us how the melodies of the wind and rain seemed to be magically transmuted into his music, so that, without any puerile attempt at direct imitation of sounds, his compositions were alive with the air of the tempest. " Son génie était plein des mystérieuses harmonies de la nature traduites par des équivalents sublimes dans sa pensée musicale, et non par une répétition servile des sons extérieurs." In Poe's genius, too, there was a kind of pre-established harmony between musical words and melancholy thoughts. As Mr. Saintsbury points out to me, though " his language not unfrequently passes from vagueness into mere unmeaningness in the literal and grammatical sense of it, yet it never fails to convey the proper suggestion in sound if not in sense. Take the lines in *Ulalume*:

> It was night in the lonesome October
> Of my most immemorial year.

Here it would puzzle the most adroit student of words to attach a distinct usual sense, authenticated by lexicons, to 'immemorial.' And yet no one with an ear can fail to see that it is emphatically the right word, and supplies the necessary note of suggestion." As to Poe's management of his metres, one cannot do better than quote Mr. Saintsbury's criticism again. "The same indefinite but intensely poetic effect is produced still more obviously by Poe's management of his metres. Every one who is acquainted with his critical work knows the care (a care that brought on him the ridicule of sciolists and poetasters) which he bestowed on metrical subjects. *The Raven, Ulalume, The Haunted Palace, Annabel Lee, For Annie*, are, each in its own way, metrical marvels, and it is not till long after we have enjoyed and admired the beauty of each as a symphony that we discern the exquisite selection and skilful juxtaposition of the parts and constituent elements of each. Every one of these remains unapproached and uncopied as a concerted piece. In *The Haunted Palace*, the metre, stately at the beginning, slackens and dies towards the close. In *Annabel Lee* and *For Annie*, on the contrary, there is a steady crescendo from first to last, while in the two other pieces the metre ebbs and flows at uncertain but skilfully arranged intervals. Poe stands almost alone in this arrangement of his lyric works as a whole. With most poets the line or the stanza is the unit, and the length of the poem is determined rather by the sense than by the sound. But with Poe the music as well as the sense (even more than the sense perhaps) is arranged and projected as a whole, nor would it be possible to curtail or omit a stanza without injuring the metrical as well as the intelligible effect."

To a critic who himself feels that the incommunicable and inexpressible charm of melodious words is of the essence of song, Poe's practice is a perpetual warning. It is to verse like Poe's, so deficient as it is in all merit but lyric music and vague emotion, so devoid of human passion—a faint rhythmical echo among stars and graves of man's laborious life—that we are reduced if we hold the theory of Poe. A critic of his own native land, Mr. Henry James, has spoken of his "valueless verse," and valueless his verse must always appear if we ask from it more than it can give. It has nothing to give but music, and people who want more must go to others that sell a different ware. We shall never appreciate Poe if we keep comparing him to men of stronger and more human natures. We must take him as one of the voices, almost the "shadow of a voice," that sound in the temple of song, and fill a little hour with music. He is not, like Homer, or Scott, or Shakespeare, or Molière, a poet that men can live with always, by the sea, in the hills, in the market-place. He is the

singer of rare hours of languor, when the soul
is vacant of the pride of life, and inclined to listen,
as it were, to the echo of a lyre from behind the hills
of death. He is like a Moschus or Bion who has
crossed the ferry and sings to Pluteus a song that
faintly reaches the ears of mortals.

$$\text{Οὐκ ἀγέραστος}$$
$$\text{ἐσσεῖθ' ἁ μολπά.}$$

" Not unrewarded " indeed is the singing, for
the verse of Poe has been prized by men with
far wider range and healthier powers than
his own.

Poe said that with him " poetry was a passion."
Yet he spoke of his own verses, in a moment of
real modesty and insight, as trifles " not of much
value to the public, or very creditable to myself."
They were, for the greater part, composed in the
most miserable circumstances, when poverty, when
neglect, when the cruel indignation of a born man
of letters, in a country where letters had not yet
won their place, were torturing the poet. He was
compelled to be a bookseller's hack. The hack's
is indeed " a damnable life," as Goldsmith said,
and was doubly or trebly damnable when *The
Bells* or *Annabel Lee* were sent the round of the
newspaper offices, to be disposed of for the price
of a dinner and a pair of boots. Poe's time was
spent in writing elaborate masterpieces for a
pittance, and in reviewing and crushing, for the
sake of bread, the productions of a crowd of

mediocrities. Then came violent and venomous quarrels, which, with enforced hackwork, devoured the energy of the poet. It is no wonder that he produced little; but even had he enjoyed happier fortunes, his range is so narrow that we could not have looked for many volumes from him. He declared that he could not and would not excite his muse, "with an eye to the paltry compensations or the more paltry commendations of mankind." Thus it may, at least, be said of him, that he was himself in his poetry, though, in writing prose, he often deserted his true inspiration. In his earlier verses he is very plainly the pupil of Shelley, as any one may see who has the courage to read through *Tamerlane* and *Al Aaraaf*. His reputation does not rest on these poems, which are longer than his own canon admitted, but on pieces of verbal music like *The Haunted Palace*, *The Sleeper*, *To One in Paradise*, *Israfel*, and the lines *To Helen*, which might be placed at the beginning of his volume. Though this beautiful piece of verse did not appear in the very earliest editions of Poe's poems, he always declared that it was written in boyhood for the woman whose death caused him, in Beddoes' phrase, "with half his heart to inhabit other worlds." Poe was well aware that his *Raven*, despite its immense popularity, was not among his best works. Indeed, it is almost too clever to be poetical, and has in it a kind of echo of Mrs. Browning, whose verse, floating in the poet's mind, probably suggested the composition. *To Helen*, *The Haunted Palace*, and *The Sleeper*, are perhaps the most coherent and powerful as well as the most melodious of Poe's verses. As his life sank in poverty, bereavement, misfortune, and misery, his verse more and more approached the vagueness of music, appealing often to mere sensation rather than to any emotion which can be stated in words. *The Bells* was written in the intervals of an unnatural lethargy; *Ulalume* scarcely pretends to remain within the limits of the poetical art, and attracts or repels by mere sounds as vacant as possible of meaning. Mr. Stedman says, truly and eloquently, that *Ulalume* " seems an improvisation, such as a violinist might play upon the instrument which had become his one thing of worth after the death of a companion who had left him alone with his own soul." The odd definition of the highest poetry as " sense swooning into nonsense " seems made for such verse as *Ulalume*. People are so constituted that, if a critic confesses his pleasure in such a thing as *Ulalume*, he is supposed to admit his inability to admire any other poetry. Thus it may require some moral courage to assert one's belief that even *Ulalume* has an excuse for its existence. It is curious and worth observing that this sort of verse is so rare. It cannot be easy to make, or the herd of imitators who approach art by its weak points would have produced quantities of this enigmatic poetry. Yet, with the exception of Poe's later verse, of Mr. Morris's *Blue Closet*, and perhaps of some pieces by Gérard de Nerval, it is difficult to name any successful lines on the further side of the border between verse and music. In this region, this "ultimate dim Thule," Poe seems to reign almost alone. The fact is that the art of hints, of fantasies, of unfinished suggestions is not an easy one, as many critics, both of poetry and painting, seem to suppose. It is not enough to be obscure, or to introduce forms unexplained and undefined. A certain very rare sort of genius is needed to make productions live which hold themselves thus independent of nature and of the rules of art. We cannot define the nature of the witchery by which the most difficult task of romantic art was achieved. Poe did succeed, as is confessed by the wide acceptance of poems that cannot be defended if any one chooses to attack them. They teach nothing, they mean little; their melody may be triumphantly explained as the result of a metrical trick. But, *ne faict ce tour qui veut*. The trick was one that only Poe could play. Like Hawthorne in prose, Poe possessed in poetry a style as strange as it was individual, a style trebly remarkable because it was the property of a hack-writer. When all is said, Poe remains a master of fantastic and melancholy sound. Some foolish old legend tells of a musician who surpassed all his rivals. His strains were unearthly sad, and ravished the ears of those who listened with a strange melancholy. Yet his viol had but a single string, and the framework was fashioned out of a dead woman's breast-bone. Poe's verse—the parallel is much in his own taste—resembles that player's minstrelsy. It is morbidly sweet and mournful, and all touched on that single string, which thrills to a dead and immortal affection.

A CYNIC'S APOLOGY

BY LESLIE STEPHEN

THERE are certain outcasts of humanity—pariahs to whom the most benevolent of mankind refuse to extend a helping hand—misshapen cripples in soul, who are displayed by some cruel demonstrator, like specimens in bottles at a medical museum, to illustrate the disastrous consequences of grievous moral disease;—and of these unfortunates I confess myself to be one. I seldom enter a church, or attend a public meeting, without hearing myself held up to execration—not by name, but by reputation—as the heartless cynic, the man who sits in the seat of the scorner, or the rightful owner of some other opprobrious title drawn from profane or sacred sources. In short, I am a person given to rather dyspeptic views of things, inclined to look at the seamy side of the world, and much more ready to laugh at a new actor than to go wild with enthusiasm over his performance. Now I freely admit that for the most part the preachers are perfectly right. Undoubtedly enthusiasm is the most essential of all qualities, if not the one thing needful. It prevents the world from sinking into a stagnant and putrefying pool. We could not improve, nor even remain in a stationary position without it. And, what is more, the preachers are justified in giving a rather exaggerated prominence to the enthusiastic view of life; for mankind is much more in want of the spur than of the curb. Let them encourage any number of young St. Georges to mount and ride forth in search of a dragon; for though in real life the dragon breed is probably extinct since the days of the pterodactyle, it will be some time before we shall want game-laws to protect dragons of the metaphorical kind, or be able to dispense with the services of any St. George that may enlist. Yet, after all, there is another side of things which we may sometimes remember when we are beyond the charmed circle of pulpit eloquence. A clergyman does well to insist chiefly upon the necessity of self-denial; but it does not follow that we should never have a taste of cakes and ale. As, indeed, we are ready enough for the most part to take our meals regularly without special encouragement, our teachers do not insist upon the necessity of our eating and drinking and indulging in an occasional festivity. They trust to the unaided propensities of our nature to secure the proper discharge of those functions, and are content to throw their whole weight upon the side of restraining our excesses. For a similar reason, I presume, we are never told that we ought sometimes to laugh at our neighbours, to throw cold water upon their zeal, and to pick holes in their favourite little projects for the reform of humanity. It is imagined that that duty may be safely left to the unprompted malevolence of our nature, of which it is presumed that there will be a sufficient crop after every diligence has been used in pruning it down. Now here, I venture to suggest, there is an omission in the common run of exhortation. There is, as I shall try to prove, a certain useful piece of work to be done, and if we are content simply to denounce those who do it, it will, of course, be done in a bad spirit and from malevolent motives. I claim no lofty mission for the cynic; and I merely suggest that, like mosquitoes, they are part of the economy of nature. One of Lincoln's apologues—of which the original application matters little—told how he and his brother were once ploughing on a Kentucky farm: the horse was going at an unusually good pace, when Lincoln knocked off a huge " chin-fly " that was fastened to his hide. " What did you do that for? " exclaimed his brother. " That's all that made him go." The whole of my claim for cynics is that they act at times the part of " chin-fly " on the pachydermatous population of the world. If we rashly attempt to crush them out of existence, we only make them more spiteful than before, and may not improbably discover that, like other vermin, they do some dirty work, which is not the essential to our comfort. The most ingenious of the socialist theorisers maintained that men who did particularly unpleasant services to mankind, should be rewarded by being held in special honour, instead of being shunned as is usual in our imperfect society. Scavengers and chimney-sweeps, for example, would have some compensation for groping in filth by occupying at other times the best seats in public places. I do not go so far as this. I am content to be trodden under foot (in spirit only) by innumerable preachers—and perhaps it does not want much courage to bear the satire of ordinary sermons; they may spit upon my gaberdine, and call me misbeliever, cut-throat dog, as much as they like. I shall never desire to cut off a pound of their flesh; I would, at most, retaliate, like poor old Shylock, by some harmless abuse, and invite them, not (as I might) to be grateful, but to remember that I too, like venomous reptiles, have a certain place in the world. To explain this a little more in detail, let us consider one or two particular cases. Thus, for example, every one who has reached a certain time of life has been annoyed by a peculiar race, known amongst its own members as the " earnest," and to the rest of mankind as prigs. It is notoriously difficult even for naturalists to trace out the identity of certain creatures who vary very much at different stages of their development. A man who remembers the companions of his university career, is sometimes amazed at the number of enthusiastic clergymen and respectable lawyers who at a later period claim to have been among his contemporaries, and wonders from what new material this finished product has been constructed. Gradually he finds that a stout boating-man, whose talk was of bumping, and whose food was of bleeding beefsteak, has fined down into an ascetic priest; or that a cadaverous mathematical student has blossomed into a rubicund lawyer. Now the case of the prig is the reverse of this. He is a specimen of arrested development. Instead of being modified by the atmosphere of the outside world, he has carried into it all the simplicity characteristic of his earliest manhood. There is something refreshing and even elevating about the spectacle of these harmless enthusiasts. They carry us back to the time when the sight of our names in a class-list produced a feeling of ineffable pride, and a fellowship seemed more glorious than a seat in the Cabinet. There is upon this earth no person who surveys mankind " from China to Peru " with a more exquisite sense of perfect complacency than the young gentleman who has just put on his bachelor's hood. Early donhood, if I may so call it, is the time of life at which nature assists us by throwing out an abnormal development of self-esteem, as the marmot grows fat to strengthen him against the approach of winter. The Union is still to our minds an assembly whose debates reverberate throughout the empire; to row in the university eight is an honour worth the sacrifice certainly of learning, and possibly even of health; to be a first-class man is to have won a decisive success in the battle of life. In the little world to which our ambition has hitherto been confined, we have risen to the summit of all things; for tutors, professors, and other authorities are nothing but contemptible old fogies, hide-bound with useless pedantry. So imposing, indeed, is the position of the youth who has just won high honours, that I confess that I have never been able to meet as an equal those who attained that position when I was a freshman. Thackeray speaks of the old gentleman of seventy who still shuddered at the dream of being flogged by the terrible headmaster of his youth. In my imagination, the lads who held sway in the university when I first had the honour of a gown, and who, as we fondly believed, rivalled, in different departments, Porson and Sir Isaac Newton, and Pitt, and Coleridge, and Byron, are still surrounded by a glory exceeding that of any of the sons of men. But a cynical freshman would be an impossible creature.

Most men soon part with their university bloom: the world demolishes their splendid ideal, and even Oxford and Cambridge sink to be provincial towns with a large proportion of cultivated men and promising lads; but not enchanted palaces of virtue and learning. The senior wrangler himself walks down the Strand without attracting a crowd; and a benighted metropolis has rather hazy notions of the precise meaning of triposes and littlegoes. Yet there are a happy few who carry about with them to later life the rose-coloured atmosphere which first gathered round them in the walks of Trinity or Christ Church, and retain the estimate then formed of the outer world of barbarians. These are the genuine prigs; and as live and let live is a very good, though very trite motto, I have no objection to their existence. They would not voluntarily hurt my feelings; and indeed the really irritating thing about them is their invariable condescension. They have the art of posing themselves like monumental statues on invisible pedestals which they carry about with them. They are sincerely anxious to put us at our ease. They smile benevolently at any little criticisms which we may hazard, as one smiles at the infantile prattle of children. They have a mission, of which they are perfectly conscious, and they move in a light not vouchsafed to the horny eyes of a cynic. But they feel deeply that their ineffable superiority does not entitle them to be harsh with us. They have even been known to approve of an occasional joke, though never condescending to make one themselves; they deal gently but firmly with us; and after we have amused ourselves with our playthings, bring us back to the discussion of a serious subject. If the conversation strays, for example, to some mere personal gossip, they take advantage of the first accidental loophole to ask our opinion of the merits of female suffrage, or the prospects of trades-unionism. On woman's rights they are especially strong—it may be from a natural sense of gratitude; for women, as natural haters of cynicisms and inclined to sentiment, are generally far more tolerant of priggishness than men. Perhaps, too, there is something pleasant to the feminine imagination in the air of infallibility which these excellent beings affect; for they are apt to gather into cliques, and round private prophets, of whom to confess ignorance is to confess yourself one of the profane. This gives them that great advantage which belongs to the esoteric disciples of a narrow sect—the power of forming mutual admiration societies. A great, though unintentional, service has been done them by an eloquent writer, as far as possible removed from their weaknesses, in popularising the nickname Philistine. Like other nicknames, that word has degenerated in common use, till it is sometimes a mere shibboleth, employed by the genuine prig to designate all who are not prigs. Not but that the two characters may be sometimes reconciled in that truly portentous variety of the prig who founds his claim to superiority on the exclusive possession of the true doctrine about the currency, or the checks and balances of the British constitution. But, as a rule, to do him justice, the prig chooses for his pet doctrine some less husky and indigestible fragment of truth.

To object to such persons in their youth would be morose; though even then the phase is not without its dangers. It implies a consciousness —which may frequently be well founded—of great powers, and a rather overweening estimate of their importance. It is useful, we may say, as the yolk which surrounds a bird before it has left the egg —on condition that it is thoroughly absorbed. When the day-dreams of the youth begin to turn into the settled delusion of the man, they first show their enervating influence. To eradicate these delusions requires that treatment with some biting social acids which cynics are destined by nature to secrete. The youthful enthusiast who has not undergone some such hardening process suffers from a sort of fatty degeneration of the moral nature. He exhibits that insipid flabby sentimentalism which does more than anything to disgust reasonable men with philanthropy. It is, doubtless, a thousand pities that any one should be disgusted with so essential a virtue: but how is it to be avoided? A man who is capable of deep emotion at the mass of misery which still stagnates in the world, who is anxious for stern and sharp remedies well considered and vigorously carried into execution, is thrust aside by the crowd of amiable quacks who are occupied in puffing themselves and their pet nostrums. The cliques—each of which possesses, in its own estimation, the one panacea for curing all our evils—form, as it were, a series of social hothouses, in which philanthropists are forced, like early peas, to an unhealthy precocity of growth. They shoot up into prize specimens, intensely admired by those who have carefully cultivated them, and

manured them with compliment and applause,
but of weak fibre and feeble constitution. If you
venture to criticise one of these gushing and
feminine creatures, you are accused of harshness,
brutality, and indifference to the finer feelings of
our nature. You are a coarse cynic, and probably
a sceptic into the bargain; your impatience of
schemes that won't work, and of feeble attempts
to varnish decayed places instead of curing them,
is considered to imply indifference to the end
desired. It is easy to set down the contempt of
practical men for half the charitable schemes of
the day to a grovelling selfishness. Much of it
may be so; but it only needs a glance at the
chaotic muddle of the London charities, to see the
advantage that would result if people would look
before they leap, and take a lesson or two from
the scorners and sneerers. Doing good requires
forethought as well as other things; and the
fashionable denunciation of cynicism has tended
to deprive us of the benefits of all criticism.
People are so charmed with the romantic aspect
of things that they won't look at the prosaic,
commonplace aspect of the evils to be encountered.
To say the truth, one is occasionally inclined to
regret that martyrdom has gone out of fashion.
Doubtless it was wrong to saw an apostle in two;
but the practice had its advantages. It forced
social reformers into a sterner temper, and a more
thorough-going policy, and discouraged the crowd
of thoughtless volunteers, who hinder the work

they profess to help. The word, indeed, remains, but its whole signification is altered. Two of the most desirable events in life are, to be suppressed by Act of Parliament or to become a martyr. In one case, you are left with a good income and nothing to do; in the other, you are the object of universal sympathy, and may very probably receive even pecuniary compensation. When stakes and faggots were in vogue, there were objections to the honour; but now it would be hard to show a man a more delicate attention than to prosecute him for heresy, whether theological, political, or even scientific, for he is certain to become a "lion," and not improbably the pet of some enthusiastic clique.

As this moral tonic has gone out of use, the critic's sneer is, perhaps, the best substitute left. It may do something to clear the atmosphere of cant, and to strip the prig of his inordinate affections. By itself it can, indeed, do nothing; but it gets rid of some of the constantly accumulating masses of humbug, and allows us at least to see things as they are. To the objection that it is cruel, the answer is that it can hardly hold the existing evils in check. The unfounded superstitution that brutal critics of a former day slew Keats by their abuse has long been worn out, and is scarcely even quoted more than once a week or so. We may say, in Rosalind's words, "men have died, and worms have eaten them" —but not of criticism. Persons who talk of the ferocity of the most fabulous creature known as the slashing critic, must indulge in some very erroneous estimates of the amount of genius in this country. A hasty calculation may be easily made. Compare the number of novelists of established reputation with the swarms of aspirants, whose first efforts are criticised in nearly every paper we take up, and then compare the number of favourable and unfavourable judgments. A rule of three will result, which would prove either that we are now turning out rivals to Fielding, or Scott, or Thackeray with unprecedented rapidity, or that many respectable writers are being welcomed with an excess of compliment. It is only too easy to say which is the most probable alternative. Or we may compare the number of living authors of recognised ability, who struggled against critics in their youth—if any such can be named— with the number who have been hopelessly spoilt by undue praise. At every turn we find really clever novelists, poets, and artists who have made a hit on their first attempt, and have ever since been their own servile imitators. It is of the rarest occurrence now to find one who has been exposed to the opposite and less searching trial of hostility, or even a want of recognition. Unless a man wilfully plunges into some abstruse branch of inquiry, some thorny byway of metaphysical or historical inquiry, he is in especially greater danger from the excess than the deficiency of sympathy. A patron, we know, in Dr. Johnson's time, was

" one who looked with unconcern on a man struggling for life in the water, and when he had reached ground, encumbered him with help." The public, we are told, has taken the place of patron and discharges it in very different fashion. It has innumerable critics placed, like the Humane Society's men on the Serpentine, with ample provision of hooks, ropes, and grapples. On the first appearance of a swimmer of any buoyancy, he is seized, hauled on shore, patted on the back, applauded, petted, treated to drinks, supplied with funds, and generally made into an idol with all the questionable advantages of such a position. If some poor critic comes by and says, " Really that young man is an impostor," he is hooted at as a cynic whose only motive must be an unworthy jealousy. And yet there are impostors—if we may imitate Galileo's profession of faith. Nay, so far is criticism from damaging genuine talent, that even an impostor, if endowed with sufficient impudence, can thrive and wax fat and sell innumerable editions in the teeth of his scorners. All that the critic can hope to do is to keep alive the belief that there is some distinction between good writing and bad, and to encourage public opinion occasionally to assert its independence. It is an encouraging fact that by incessantly hammering at the point, sensation novelists have been forced to put forward a defence. Critics are totally unable to crush the faults of which they complain, but they can maintain a certain sensibility to blame. It is still known by tradition that there are some canons of good taste, which a man may indeed safely defy so far as his bookseller's account is concerned, but which will avenge themselves on his future fame. If the tradition does not quite expire, it is due to a few faithful critics—much reviled by the enthusiastic part of mankind—who go about smiting pretenders right and left; and, it may be, sometimes administering a random blow to some one who does not deserve it.

The enthusiasts, who think that revolutions are to be made with rosewater, that the world is to be awed by patting all the good boys on the head without administering the birch to the bad ones, may possibly object to this doctrine. It sounds plausible to say, praise the good and let the bad find its own path to decay. Yet even they will perhaps admit some force in the next claim which I venture to put forward. There are in this world certain persons known by the good old English name of fools. Although we shrink from applying the name to any individual, we know that, in the aggregate, they form a vast and almost impenetrable phalanx. Like other men, they have their uses; they serve, perhaps, as ballast, and prevent the machinery of the world from moving too fast. Certainly they do it effectually. There is something portentous about the huge masses of dogged stupidity which environ us on every side. There are noodles alive who repeat with infinite variations the oration composed for them by Sydney

Smith, and repeat their little saws about the wisdom of our ancestors, the contrast between theory and practice, and other profound considerations leading up to the grand conclusion, *Nolumus leges Angliæ mutari.* It may be that some of the finest specimens of the tribe were those who lately engaged in the defence of the worst abuses in workhouses, and happily compared all who denounced them to persons with a morbid appetite for " putrid oysters." The force of the analogy may not be very obvious, but it had a certain currency at the time from the happy confusion of ideas which it indicated. Vestrymen, as this scrap of their eloquence implies, are frequently dull; and it may even be that their education gives them a dullness of a peculiarly fine flavour. But we cannot flatter ourselves that dullness is confined to Bumbledom, nor to its unfortunate subjects. There is, we may venture to imagine, some stupidity in high places; and if any doubts be entertained on the subject, we might ask Mr. Mill for his opinion of Conservative members of Parliament, or Mr. Bright for his views of bishops. Assuming that those eminent men cannot be speaking entirely without book, and noting, for our private edification, the singular resemblance between the two sides of the House of Commons, and the fact that lawn sleeves do not naturally change human nature, we may venture to hazard a conjecture that there is probably a good deal of stupidity up and down the country. How is it to be assaulted with any prospect of success? The thick armour which Providence has bestowed upon this class of mankind is proverbial. Take it for a rule, as the poet observes,

> No creature smarts so little as a fool.

But if anything is to be done, he must be made to smart. Some one must do for him that kind office which had to be done for the mediæval knight who had been tumbled over in his impregnable suit of armour, and force open the rivets. Where is his vulnerable place? Preaching, however eloquent, passes over him like a distant and pleasant murmur. He plants himself more firmly in his seat, and refuses to budge. He is like a huge wrestler whom I have seen wearing down his active antagonist by sheer weight. If he moved, he was thrown in an instant; but so long as he stood stolidly stockstill no efforts were of the slightest use. We want some one to stir him up as the Spanish bull is excited by a firework or two planted in his neck. Now, fortunately, the very dullest of mortals is more or less accessible to contempt. He dislikes being written down an ass. He throws off his mantle of sevenfold indifference under a few judicious taunts, and brings his clumsy strength into the arena. It is curious to remark how, in a political contest, the loftiest eloquence loses its effect after a day or two; and some little epigram thrown out in the heat of the contest remains fizzing and sparkling unquenchably, in spite of all efforts to stamp it out, and keeps up the spirit of the weary combatants. Keen, scornful common sense, compressed into a few pungent words, piercing through the buncombe and the flummery, should be welcomed even by those it attacks. It is the signal that the parade of the fencer with blunted foils is over, and that real work with sharp steel is beginning.

But it may be urged this is, after all, a debasing view of things. Cynics who delight to pierce wind-bags and to unmask humbugs, are equally apt to throw mud at heroes. Even if the hero laughs at them, the popular mind is prejudiced. If, in those old days of dragons and martyrs, there had been such things as newspaper reporters and weekly essayists, what kind of criticism would have greeted men who died in the discharge of the noblest of duties? Or suppose that even now some gallant missionary has been devoured in the Cannibal Islands, and that the court journalist of that country has managed to catch something of the European tone. "The news which has just come to us," he would perhaps say, "is certainly to be lamented. Cannibalism, as a custom, is undoubtedly doomed, though we may regret the sentimentality which has finally suppressed so picturesque and harmless a custom. Be that as it may, we have become too dainty to eat our enemies, though not too dainty to kill them; we have sacrificed to morbid prejudices a savoury and nutritious article of diet; and, of course, laws,

however unsatisfactory in point of reason, must be
obeyed. Even missionaries who land upon our
shores must be protected. But we would ask them,
if they still retain any gleams of common sense,
what it is that they expect to gain? Mumbo
Jumbo may not be in all respects a satisfactory
object of worship; but what known doctrine is
thoroughly satisfactory? His worshippers believe
that if they knock each other on the head, or marry
more than a dozen wives, or eat human flesh out
of season, they will suffer for it; it is a rough
creed containing, it may be, some errors; but, on
the whole, it is excellently adapted to the state of
civilisation, and any more refined doctrines would
simply fly over the people's heads. Mumbo
Jumbo's priests are not men of any high polish,
but they have a great influence over the vulgar,
and save some expense in police arrangements.
The man who upsets such a state of things, incurs
a heavy responsibility, and ought to be perfectly
clear that his teaching will be better adapted to
the minds of his audience. If he is fool enough,
for the sake of so doubtful a good, to run the risk
of being made into chops, we are of course bound,
as far as may be, to frustrate his excellent
intention, and to prevent him from obtaining
the object of his foolish wishes. So far as we
can secure it by reasonable precautions, his friends
shall not boast that he has been converted
into meat, roast, boiled, or baked; but if
we unluckily fail, they must also thoroughly

understand that we hold him to be simply an idiot whose folly has met with its natural, if not its lawful reward."

In some such tone, I imagine, we should greet many martyrdoms nowadays: and I fully admit that it is only within narrow bounds, only when acting as a strictly subordinate check, that cynicism is desirable or pardonable. Mustard is a good thing, but we cannot dine off it; and there are, undoubtedly, limits to the use of vitriol. When chivalry is sneered away, there is a fearful loss to the people whose powers of reverence are injured; only at present I fear it is in equal danger of being stifled by injudicious praise, and lost from sight in a mass of Brummagem imitations. A little supply of cynicism should be kept on hand to test the genuine nature of the article. Let us only reflect, to use one obvious illustration, how much good would be done if in every church there came in at sermon-time the cynic who is so often denounced in his absence; if he was accommodated with a seat, and allowed to put the clergyman a few questions afterwards in private: would not the logic to which we are treated be generally sounder, the eloquence more severe, and a little more care be shown not to shelter sheer nonsense under the respect due to sacred things? We should, I fancy, more frequently enjoy what, in spite of all that is said against sermons, is really one of the most elevating of all possible influences, the eloquence of a man who has put the whole powers of his mind to enforce doctrines of whose truth and vital importance he is even passionately convinced, and who further remembers that he is talking to men as well as to children.

CATS [1]

By Edmund Gosse

An accomplished lady of my acquaintance tells me that she is preparing an anthology of the cat. This announcement has reminded me of one of the oddest and most entertaining volumes in my library. People who collect prints of the eighteenth century know an engraving which represents a tom-cat, rampant, holding up an oval portrait of a gentleman and standing, in order to do so, on a volume. The volume is *Les Chats*, the book before us, and the portrait is that of the author, the amiable and amusing Augustin Paradis de Moncrif. He was the son of English, or more probably of Scotch parents settled in Paris, where he was born in 1687. All we know of his earlier years is to be found in a single sparkling page of d'Alembert, who makes Moncrif float out of obscurity like the most elegant of iridescent bubbles. He was handsome and seductive, turned a copy of verses with the best of gentlemen, but was particularly distinguished by the art with

[1] *Les Chats*. A Rotterdam, chez Jean Daniel Beman, MDCCXXVII.

which he purveyed little dramas for the amateur stage, then so much in fashion in France. Somebody said of him, when he was famous as the laureate of the cats, that he had risen in life by never scratching, by always having velvet paws, and by never putting up his back, even when he was startled. Voltaire called him " my very dear Sylph," and he was the ideal of all that was noiseless, graceful, good-humoured, and well-bred. He slipped unobtrusively into the French Academy, and lived to be eighty-three, dying at last, like Anacreon, in the midst of music and dances and fair nymphs of the Opera, affecting to be a sad old rogue to the very last.

This book on Cats, the only one by which he is now remembered, was the sole production of his lifetime which cost him any annoyance. He was forty years of age when it appeared, and the subject was considered a little frivolous, even for such a *petit conteur* as Moncrif. People continued to tease him about it, and the only rough thing he ever did was the result of one such twitting. The poet Roy made an epigram about " cats " and " rats," in execrable taste, no doubt; this stung our Sylph to such an excess that he waited outside the Palais Royal and beat Roy with a stick when he came out. The poet was, perhaps, not much hurt; at all events, he had the presence of mind to retort, " Patte de velours, patte de velours, Minon-minet ! " It was six years after this that Moncrif was elected into the French

Academy, and then the shower of epigrams broke
out again. He wished to be made historiographer;
"Oh, nonsense," the wits cried, "he must mean
historiogriffe," and they invited him, on nights
when the Academy met, to climb on to the roof
and miau from the chimney-pots. He had the
weakness to apologise for his charming book, and
to withdraw it from circulation. His pastoral tales
and heroic ballets, his *Zélindors* and *Zéloïdes* and
Erosines, which to us seem and are utterly vapid
and frivolous, never gave him a moment's un-
easiness. His crumpled roseleaf was the book by
which his name lives in literature.

The book of cats is written in the form of eleven
letters to Madame la Marquise de B——. The
anonymous author represents himself as too much
excited to sleep, after an evening spent in a fashionable house, where the company was abusing cats.
He was unsupported; where was the Marquise,
who would have brought a thousand arguments
to his assistance, founded on her own experience
of virtuous pussies? Instead of going to bed he
will sit up and indite the panegyric of the feline
race. He is still sore at the prejudice and injustice
of the people he has just left. It culminated in the
conduct of a lady who declared that cats were
poison, and who, "when pussy appeared in the
room, had the presence of mind to faint." These
people had rallied him on the absurdity of his
enthusiasm; but, as he says, the Marquise well
knows, "how many women have a passion for

cats, and how many men are women in this respect."

So he starts away on his dissertation, with all its elegant pedantry, its paradoxical wit, its genuine touches of observation and its constant sparkle of anecdote. He is troubled to account for the existence of the cat. An Ottoman legend relates that when the animals were in the Ark, Noah gave the lion a great box on the ear, which made him sneeze, and produce a cat out of his nose. But the author questions this origin, and is more inclined to agree with a Turkish Minister of Religion, sometime Ambassador to France, that the ape, " weary of a sedentary life " in the Ark, paid his attentions to a very agreeable young lioness, whose infidelities resulted in the birth of a Tom-cat and a Puss-cat, and that these, combining the qualities of their parents, spread through the Ark *un esprit de coquetterie*—which lasted during the whole of the sojourn there. Moncrif has no difficulty in showing that the East has always been devoted to cats, and he tells the story of Mahomet, who, being consulted one day on a point of piety, preferred to cut off his sleeve, on which his favourite pussy was asleep, rather than wake her violently by rising.

From the French poets, Moncrif collects a good many curious tributes to the " harmless, necessary cat." I am seized with an ambition to put some fragments of these into English verse. Most of them are highly complimentary. It is true that

Ronsard was one of those who could not appreciate
a "matou." He sang or said:

> There is no man now living anywhere
>   Who hates cats with a deeper hate than I;
> I hate their eyes, their heads, the way they stare,
>   And when I see one come, I turn and fly.

But among the *précieuses* of the seventeenth
century there was much more appreciation. Mme.
Deshoulières wrote a whole series of songs and
couplets about her cat, Grisette. In a letter to
her husband, referring to the attentions she herself
receives from admirers, she adds:

> Deshoulières cares not for the smart
>   Her bright eyes cause, disdainful hussy,
> But, like a mouse, her idle heart
>   Is captured by a pussy.

Much better than these is the sonnet on the cat
of the Duchess of Lesdiguières, with its admirable
line:

> Chatte pour tout le monde, et pour les chats tigresse.

A fugitive epistle by Scarron, delightfully
turned, is too long to be quoted here, nor can
I pause to cite the rondeau which the Duchess
of Maine addressed to her favourite. But she
supplemented it as follows:

> My pretty puss, my solace and delight,
> To celebrate thy loveliness aright
> I ought to call to life the bard who sung
> Of Lesbia's sparrow with so sweet a tongue;
> But 'tis in vain to summon here to me
> So famous a dead personage as he,
> And you must take contentedly to-day
> This poor rondeau that Cupid wafts your way.

When this cat died the Duchess was too much affected to write its epitaph herself, and accordingly it was done for her, in the following style, by La Mothe le Vayer, the author of the *Dialogues*:

> Puss passer-by, within this simple tomb
>   Lies one whose life fell Atropos hath shred;
> The happiest cat on earth hath heard her doom,
>   And sleeps for ever in a marble bed.
> Alas! what long delicious days I've seen!
>   O cats of Egypt, my illustrious sires,
> You who on altars, bound with garlands green,
>   Have melted hearts, and kindled fond desires,—
> Hymns in your praise were paid, and offerings too,
>   But I'm not jealous of those rights divine,
> Since Ludovisa loved me, close and true,
>   Your ancient glory was less proud than mine.
> To live a simple pussy by her side
> Was nobler far than to be deified.

To these and other tributes Moncrif adds idylls and romances of his own, while regretting that it never occurred to Theocritus to write a *bergerie de chats*. He tells stories of blameless pussies beloved by Fontenelle and La Fontaine, and quotes Marot in praise of " the green-eyed Venus." But he tears himself away at last from all these historical reminiscences, and in his eleventh letter he deals with cats as they are. We hasten as lightly as possible over a story of the disinterestedness of a feline Héloise, which is too pathetic for a nine-teenth-century era. But we may repeat the touch-ing anecdote of Bayle's friend, Mlle. Dupuy. This lady excelled to a surprising degree in playing the harp, and she attributed her excellence in this accomplishment to her cat, whose critical taste was only equalled by his close attention to Mlle. Dupuy's performance. She felt that she owed so much to this cat, under whose care her reputation for skill on the harp had become universal, that when she died she left him, in her will, one agreeable house in town and another in the country. To this bequest she added a revenue sufficient to supply all the requirements of a well-bred tom-cat, and at the same time she left pensions to certain persons whose duty it should be to wait upon him. Her ignoble family contested the will, and there was a long suit. Moncrif gives a handsome double-plate illustration of this incident. Mlle. Dupuy, sadly wasted by illness, is seen in bed, with her cat in her arms, dictating her will to the family lawyer in a periwig; her physician is also present.

This leads me to speak of the illustrations to *Les Chats*, which greatly add to its value. They were engraved by Otten from original drawings by Coypel. In another edition the same drawings are engraved by Count Caylus. Some of them are of a charming absurdity. One, a double plate, represents a tragedy acted by cats on the roof of a fashionable house. The actors are tricked out in the most magnificent feathers and furbelows, but the audience consists of common cats. Cupid sits above, with his bow and fluttering wings. Another plate shows the mausoleum of the Duchess of Lesdiguière's cat, with a marble pussy of heroic size, upon a marble pillow, in a grove of poplars.

Another is a medal to " Chat Noir premier, né en 1725," with the proud inscription, " Knowing to whom I belong, I am aware of my value." The profile within is that of as haughty a tom as ever shook out his whiskers in a lady's boudoir.

CHRISTOPHER SMART [1]

By Edmund Gosse

THE third section of Mr. Browning's *Parleyings with certain People of Importance in their Day* has drawn general attention to a Cambridge poet of whom little has hitherto been known, Christopher Smart, once fellow of Pembroke College. It may be interesting, therefore, to supply some sketch of the events of his life, and of the particular poem which Mr. Browning has aptly compared to a gorgeous chapel lying *perdue* in a dull old common-place mansion. No one can afford to be entirely indifferent to the author of verses which one of the greatest of modern writers has declared to be unequalled of their kind between Milton and Keats.

What has hitherto been known of the facts of Smart's life has been founded on the anonymous biography prefixed to the two-volume Reading edition of his works, published in 1791. The copy of this edition in Trinity Library belonged to Dr. Farmer, and contains these words in his hand-

[1] *Poems on Several Occasions.* By Christopher Smart, A.M., Fellow of Pembroke-Hall, Cambridge. London: Printed for the Author, by W. Strahan; And sold by J. Newbery, at the Bible and Sun, in St. Paul's Church-yard. MDCCLII.

writing, " From the Editor, Francis Newbery, Esq.;
the Life by Mr. Hunter." As this Newbery was the
son of Smart's half-brother-in-law and literary
employer, it may be taken for granted that the
information given in these volumes is authoritative.
We may therefore believe it to be correct that
Smart was born (as he himself tells us, in *The
Hop Garden*) at Shipbourne, in Kent, on the 11th
of April 1722, that his father was steward to the
nobleman who afterwards became Earl of Darling-
ton, and that he was " discerned and patronised "
by the Duchess of Cleveland. This great lady, we
are left in doubt for what reason, carried her
complaisance so far as to allow the future poet
£40 a year until her death. In a painfully fulsome
ode to another member of the Raby Castle family,
Smart records the generosity of the dead in order
to stimulate that of the living, and oddly remarks
that

> dignity itself restrains
> By condescension's silken reins,
> While you the lowly Muse upraise.

Smart passed, already " an infant bard," from
what he calls " the splendour in retreat " of Raby
Castle, to Durham School, and in his eighteenth
year was admitted of Pembroke Hall, October 30,
1739. His biographer expressly states that his
allowance from home was scanty, and that his
chief dependence, until he derived an income from
his college, was on the bounty of the Duchess of
Cleveland.

From this point I am able to supply a certain amount of information with regard to the poet's college life which is entirely new, and which is not, I think, without interest. My friend Mr. R. A. Neil has been so kind as to admit me to the Treasury at Pembroke, and in his company I have had the advantage of searching the contemporary records of the college. What we were lucky enough to discover may here be briefly summarised. The earliest mention of Smart is dated 1740, and refers to the rooms assigned to him as an undergraduate. In January 1743, we find him taking his B.A., and in July of the same year he is elected scholar. As is correctly stated in his Life he became a fellow of Pembroke on the 3rd of July 1745. That he showed no indication as yet of that disturbance of brain and instability of character which so painfully distinguished him a little later on, is proved by the fact that on the 10th of October 1745, Smart was chosen to be Prælector in Philosophy, and Keeper of the Common Chest. In 1746 he was re-elected to those offices, and also made Prælector in Rhetoric. In 1747 he was not chosen to hold any such college situations, no doubt from the growing extravagance of his conduct.

In November 1747, Smart was in parlous case. Gray complains of his " lies, impertinence and ingratitude," and describes him as confined to his room, lest his creditors should snap him up. He gives a melancholy impression of Smart's moral

and physical state, but hastens to add " not that
I, nor any other mortal, pity him." The records
of the Treasury at Pembroke supply evidence that
the members of the college now made a great
effort to restore one of whose talents it is certain
they were proud. In 1748 we find Smart proposed
for catechist, a proof that he had, at all events for
the moment, turned over a new leaf. Probably,
but for fresh relapses, he would now have taken
orders. His allusions to college life are singularly
ungracious. He calls Pembroke

> this servile cell,
> Where discipline and dulness dwell,

and commiserates a captive eagle as being doomed
in the college courts to watch

> Scholastic pride
> Take his precise, pedantic stride;

words which painfully remind us of Gray's reported
manner of enjoying a constitutional. It is certain
that there was considerable friction between these
two men of genius, and Gray roundly prophesied
that Smart would find his way to gaol or to Bedlam.
Both alternatives of this prediction were fulfilled,
and in October 1751, Gray curtly remarks : " Smart
sets out for Bedlam." Of this event we find curious
evidence in the Treasury. " October 12, 1751.—
Ordered that Mr. Smart, being obliged to be
absent, there will be allowed him in lieu of
commons for the year ended Michaelmas, 1751,
the sum of £10." There can be little question that

Smart's conduct and condition became more and more unsatisfactory. This particular visit to a madhouse was probably brief, but it was possibly not the first and was soon repeated; for in 1749 and in 1752 there are similar entries recording the fact that," Mr. Smart being obliged to be absent," certain allowances were paid by the college " in consideration of his circumstances." The most curious discovery, however, which we have been able to make is recorded in the following entry:

" Nov. 27, 1753.—Ordered that the dividend assigned to Mr. Smart be deposited in the Treasury till the Society be satisfied that he has a right to the same; it being credibly reported that he has been married for some time, and that notice be sent to Mr. Smart of his dividend being detained."

As a matter of fact, Smart was by this time married to a relative of Newbery, the publisher, for whom he was doing hack work in London. He had, however, formed the habit of writing the Seatonian prize poem, which he had already gained four times, in 1750, 1751, 1752, and 1753. He seems to have clutched at the distinction which he brought on his college by these poems as the last straw by which to keep his fellowship, and, singular to say, he must have succeeded; for on the 16th of January 1754, this order was recorded:

" That Mr. Smart have leave to keep his name in the college books without any expense, so long as he continues to write for the premium left by Mr. Seaton."

How long this inexpensive indulgence lasted does not seem to be known. Smart gained the Seatonian prize in 1755, having apparently failed in 1754, and then appears no more in Pembroke records.

The circumstances of his having made Cambridge too hot to hold him seems to have pulled Smart's loose faculties together. The next five years were probably the sanest and the busiest in his life. He had collected his scattered odes and ballads, and published them, with his ambitious georgic, *The Hop Garden*, in the handsome quarto before us. Among the seven hundred subscribers to this venture we find " Mr. Voltaire, historiographer of France," and M. Roubilliac, the great statuary, besides such English celebrities as Gray, Collins, Richardson, Savage, Charles Avison, Garrick, and Mason. The kind reception of this work awakened in the poet an inordinate vanity, which found expression, in 1753, in that extraordinary effusion, *The Hilliad*, an attempt to present Dr. John Hill in such amber as Pope held at the command of his satiric passion. But these efforts, and an annual Seatonian, were ill adapted to support a poet who had recently appended a wife and family to a phenomenal appetite for strong waters, and who, moreover, had just been deprived of his stipend as a fellow. Smart descended into Grub Street, and bound himself over, hand and foot, to be the serf of such men as the publisher Newbery, who was none the milder master for being his relative. It was not long after, doubtless, that Smart fell lower still, and let himself out on a lease for ninety-nine years, to toil for a set pittance in the garrets of Gardner's shop; and it was about this time, 1754, that the Rev. T. Tyers was introduced to Smart by a friend who had more sympathy with his frailties than Gray had, namely, Dr. Samuel Johnson.

After a world of vicissitudes, which are very uncomfortable reading, about 1761 Smart became violently insane once more and was shut up again in Bedlam. Dr. Johnson, commenting on this period of the poet's life, told Dr. Burney that Smart grew fat when he was in the madhouse, where he dug in the garden, and Johnson added: "I did not think he ought to be shut up. His infirmities were not noxious to society. He insisted on people praying with him; and I'd as lief pray with Kit Smart as with any one else. Another charge was that he did not love clean linen; and I have no passion for it." When Boswell paid Johnson his memorable first visit in 1763, Smart had recently been released from Bedlam, and Johnson naturally spoke of him. He said: "My poor friend Smart showed the disturbance of his mind by falling upon his knees and saying his prayers in the street, or in any other unusual place." Gray about the same time reports that money is being collected to help " poor Smart," not for the first time, since in January 1759, Gray had written: " Poor Smart is not dead, as was said, and *Merope* is acted for his benefit this week," with the *Guardian*, a farce which Garrick had kindly composed for that occasion.

It was in 1763, immediately after Smart's release, that the now famous *Song to David* was published. A long and interesting letter in the correspondence of Hawkesworth, dated October 1764, gives a pleasant idea of Smart restored to cheerfulness and placed " with very decent people in a house, most delightfully situated, with a terrace that overlooks St. James's Park." But this relief was only temporary; Smart fell back presently into drunkenness and debt, and was happily relieved by death in 1770, in his forty-eighth year, at the close of a career as melancholy as any recorded in the chronicles of literature.

Save for one single lyric, that glows with all the flush and bloom of Eden, Smart would take but a poor place on the English Parnassus. His odes and ballads, his psalms and satires, his masques and his georgics, are not bad, but they are mediocre. Here and there the very careful reader may come across lines and phrases that display the concealed author of the *Song to David*, such as the following, from an excessively tiresome ode to Dr. Webster:

> When Israel's host, with all their stores,
> Passed through *the ruby-tinctured crystal shores,*
> *The wilderness of waters and of land.*

But these are rare. His odes are founded upon those of Gray, and the best that can be said of them is that if they do not quite rise to the frozen elegance of Akenside, they seldom sink to the flaccidity of Mason. Never, for one consecutive stanza or stroke, do they approach Collins or Gray in delicacy or power. But the *Song to David*—the lyric in 516 lines which Smart is so absurdly fabled to have scratched with a key on the white-washed walls of his cell—this was a portent of beauty and originality. Strange to say, it was utterly neglected when it appeared, and the editor of the 1791 edition of Smart's works expressly omitted to print it on the ground that it bore too many "melancholy proofs of the estrangement of Smart's mind" to be fit for republication. It became rare to the very verge of extinction, and is now scarcely to be found in its entirety save in a pretty reprint of 1819, itself now rare, due to the piety of a Rev. R. Harvey.

It is obvious that Smart's contemporaries and immediate successors looked upon the *Song to David* as the work of a hopelessly deranged person. In 1763 poetry had to be very sane indeed to be attended to. The year preceding had welcomed the *Shipwreck* of Falconer, the year to follow would welcome Goldsmith's *Traveller* and Grainger's *Sugar Cane*, works of various merit, but all eminently sane. In 1763 Shenstone was dying and Rogers was being born. The tidy, spruce and discreet poetry of the eighteenth century was passing into its final and most pronounced stage. The *Song to David*, with its bold mention of unfamiliar things, its warm and highly coloured phraseology, its daring adjectives and unexampled adverbs, was an outrage upon taste, and one which was best accounted for by the tap of the forefinger on the forehead. No doubt the poem presented and still may present legitimate difficulties. Here, for instance, is a stanza which it is not for those who run to read:

> Increasing days their reign exalt,
> Nor in the pink and mottled vault
> The opposing spirits tilt;
> And, by the coasting reader spy'd,
> The silverlings and crusions glide
> For Adoration gilt.

This is charming; but if it were in one of the tongues of the heathen we should get Dr. Verrall to explain it away. Poor Mr. Harvey, the editor of 1819, being hopelessly puzzled by " silverlings," the only dictionary meaning of which is " shekels," explained " crusions " to be some other kind of money, from κροῦσις. But " crusions " are golden carp, and when I was a child the Devonshire fishermen used to call the long white fish with argent stripes (whose proper name, I think, is the launce) a silverling. The " coasting reader " is the courteous reader when walking along the coast, and what he sees are silver fish and gold fish, adoring the Lord by the beauty of their scales. The *Song to David* is cryptic to a very high degree, but I think there are no lines in it which patient reflection will not solve. On every page are stanzas the verbal

splendour of which no lover of poetry will question,
and lines which will always, to me at least, retain
an echo of that gusto with which I have heard Mr.
Browning's strong voice recite them:

> The wealthy crops of whitening rice
> 'Mongst thyine woods and groves of spice,
>   For Adoration grow;
> And, marshall'd in the fencèd land,
> The peaches and pomegranates stand,
>   Where wild carnations blow.
>
> The laurels with the winter strive;
> The crocus burnishes alive
>   Upon the snow-clad earth;
>
> .   .   .   .   .
>
> For Adoration ripening canes
> And cocoa's purest milk detains
>   The western pilgrim's staff;
> Where rain in clasping boughs inclos'd,
> And vines with oranges dispos'd,
>   Embower the social laugh.
>
> For Adoration, beyond match,
> The scholar bulfinch aims to catch
>   The soft flute's ivory touch;
> And, careless on the hazle spray,
> The daring redbreast keeps at bay
>   The damsel's greedy touch.

To quote at further length from so fascinating,
so divine a poem, would be " purpling too much
my mere grey argument." Mr. Browning's praise
ought to send every one to the original. But here
is one more stanza that I cannot resist copying,
because it seems so pathetically applicable to
Smart himself as a man, and to the one exquisite

poem which was " the more than Abishag of his age ":

> His muse, bright angel of his verse,
> Gives balm for all the thorns that pierce,
> For all the pangs that rage;
> Blest light, still gaining on the gloom,
> The more than Michal of his bloom,
> The Abishag of his age.

A BELT OF ASTEROIDS

By Edmund Clarence Stedman

Now and then a name becomes durably known in literature through the reputation of a single fugitive poem. Our English lyrical system has, of course, its greater and lesser planets, with their groups of attendant satellites. At irregular periods, some comet flashes into view, lights up the skies for a time, and then disappears beyond the vision. Whether, after the completion of a cycle, it will again attract attention and become an accepted portion of this solar family, or whether, being of a transient though garish presence, it will lessen forever upon its hyperbolic skyway, cannot always be determined by observers. And lastly, at the risk of tearing a metaphor to tatters, I may say that there are scattered through certain intervals of the system, like those fragments between the orbits of Jupiter and Mars, the asteroidal poets, each of whom we have recognised by a single and distinctive point of light.

The one effort of an amateur is accepted by the people, or gains favour with compilers who select and preserve whatever is of lasting value. The result is a wide public knowledge of these kinless poems, and of the facts which have attended their begetting; so that I shall not hunt for new matter, or reason too curiously upon my theme. Rather let me associate a few of the best-known and even hackneyed pieces of this sort, while the reader considers the philosophy of their production and success.

One is tempted to borrow a title from the British politicians, who, as everybody knows, called a member of Parliament " Single-Speech Hamilton," after his delivery of a sound and persuasive harangue upon the finances, in November 1775. If the essence of fun be incongruity, then the nickname was not amiss, for it was certainly incongruous and odd that a member, who had dozed through silent terms, should jump up at a crisis and add unexpected strength to his party by the eloquence of a trained rhetorician and a wisdom which none dreamed he could possess. I have no doubt that, before morning, at the clubs, hundreds and fifties were offered against his ever speaking again. If so, he must have become as obnoxious to those who took the odds as were the portly old buffers who darkened coffee-house windows long beyond the dates at which the younger bucks had wagered that apoplexy would seize them; for Hamilton, having once tasted renown, did, it seems, essay more speeches, thereby putting the nicknamers and gamesters to confusion; which leads De Quincey to remark, with a chuckle over the whimsies of humanity, that the generation " had greatly esteemed the man called Single-Speech Hamilton, not at all for the speech (which, though good, very few people had read), but entirely from the supposed fact that he had exhausted himself in one speech, and had been physically incapable of making a second; so that afterward, when he did make a second, everybody was incredulous, until, the thing being demonstrated, naturally the world was disgusted, and most people dropped his acquaintance."

The world is thus jealous of its preconceived opinions, or of rivalry to an established favourite, and will always array the old against the new. It begrudges a chance hand the right to hit the bull's-eye more than once, and measures each successive shot with unkind exactness; so that only those who have the root of the matter in them, and do better and better, are at all advanced by fresh trials after one triumph. A first achievement will be merged, and thought even less of, among equal others of the kind.

That was a shrewder fellow, of our own day and country, who took warning from Hamilton's misfortunes, and delivered *his* single speech at the close of a long Senatorial term, knowing that the loss of an election had put him beyond the perils of anti-climax. Sitting at his desk—he had been a cripple for years—and talking off his speech in the most random manner, he was logical and humorous by turns, drove black care from the

Senate Chamber, and threw a singularly grotesque glamour over the last night of that doleful session which preceded the opening of our civil war. Next morning he left in a blaze of glory for Kentucky, and, so far as I know, was never heard of more.

Our business, however, is not with the politicians, but with that superior race, the poets. Not that these songsters are exempted from a common law. If, once in a while, some brown domestic bird varies his wonted piping, and breaks out in passionate and melodious notes; or, when a brilliant-plumed creature, kept rather for ornament than song, seems to have borrowed the throstle's minstrelsy—if these venture again, the one must have lighter trills and quavers, and the other a purer and more assured sweetness, or it will be said of each that

> —he never could recapture
> The first fine careless rapture.

Many a second performance has thus been stifled within the hearing of us all.

He who has discerned and made available the one fortunate moment of his life, has not lived entirely in vain. Multitudes pass through the sacred garden unawares, with their eyes fixed upon illusions far away. Yet there comes to most persons a time when they are lifted above the hard level of common life to the region of spiritual emotion and discovery. The dullest eye will catch glimpses to make one less forlorn; the

ear will be suddenly unsealed, and hear the bells
of heaven ring; the mouth will be touched with
fire, and utter imaginative speech. Were there not
something divine in each of us, a poet would find
no listeners. Thus the crises of passion, joy and
pain, which are inevitable for all, often raise the
most plodding to a comprehension of the rapture
of the poet, the devotion of the martyr, the assur-
ance of the leader of his kind. The clear vision
demands, and for the moment seems to carry with
it, a new gift of expression. Men speak with
tongues they never knew before; yet, when the
Pentecost is over, relapse into their ordinary existence, and wonder no less than others at what it
has been given them to do.

A chance lyric composed in this wise, and the
sole performance which has interested the world
in its author, has frequently seemed to the latter
so light a thing that he has neglected to identify
his name with its success. Scores of the ballads
which mark the growth of our English poetry, and
are now gathered and edited as a portion of its
history, have given no fame to the minor poets
who sang them,

> Ere days that deal in *ana* swarmed
> Their literary leeches.

Doubtless not a few of those notable anonymous
pieces, which people love to attribute to some
favourite author or hero, have been, could we only
determine it, the single productions of amateurs.

There is *The Lye*, for example, which is claimed
for Sir Walter Raleigh, and is quite good enough
for him to have written—is better than anything
established as his own—yet whose authorship is
still in escrow between Raleigh, Sylvester, and
others of less repute. There are some plaintive
stanzas, which commence " Defiled is my name
full sore," and profess to be the lament of Queen
Ann Boleyn from her prison cell, but are undoubtedly the work of another hand. The lovers
of that soldierly canticle, *How Stands the Glass
Around?* indignant that so lusty and winsome
a child should be a foundling, have tried to fix
its paternity upon General James Wolfe, because
that chivalrous Englisher delighted in it, and used
to troll it melodiously across the board. This
catch, more widely recognised by the second
stanza—

> Why, soldiers, why
> Should you be melancholy, boys?
> Why, soldiers, why,
> Whose business 'tis to die?—

is indeed the perfection of a soldier's banqueting
song—not only pathetic and musical, but with
cadences of rhythm so adjusted that it has a
pulsing accent at intervals which relate to the
drum-beat and the martial tread of ranks. Any
poet might be glad to have composed it. We
have it, as copied from a half-sheet of music
printed about the year 1710. Perhaps it was
brought over from the Low Countries by Marl-

borough's men; yet there is the ring of Dryden's measures about it, and a poet, whose instinct upon such matters is almost unfailing, has declared to me that he would venture to ascribe it to glorious John upon this internal evidence alone. The authors of a hundred comparatively modern ballads and ditties, like *The Children in the Wood, Comin' thro' the Rye, When this Old Cap was New*, have left their voices alone behind them; yet each voice seems to have a distinctive quality of its own. Who wrote *The White Rose*, that darling little conceit of a Yorkist lover to his Lancastrian mistress? The twin stanzas have become a jewel upon the "stretched fore-finger of all time." James Somerville laid violent hands upon them, early in the last century, remodelled them, and added three verses of his own, each weaker than the predecessor. It has been the fate of many pretty wanderers to be thus kidnapped and rechristened, and sometimes, fortunately, by nobler craft than Somerville's, to be changed to something truly rich and rare. As when John Milton based *Il Penseroso* upon the verses *In Praise of Melancholy*, commencing:

> Hence, all ye vain delights!

and ending:

> Here stretch our bones in a still, gloomy valley,
> Nothing's so dainty sweet as lovely melancholy.

These have been claimed for Fletcher, since he inserted them in his play of *The Nice Valour*, but possibly were composed by Dr. William Strode, who flourished in the first half of the seventeenth century. Dr. Strode is also thought to have written a lyric often quoted as Dryden's, *The Commendation of Music*, which contains some delicate lines:

> Oh, lull me, lull me, charming air,
> My senses rocked with wonder sweet!
> Like snow on wool thy fallings are,
> Soft like a spirit are thy feet.

Campbell found the key-note of his resonant naval ode, *Ye Mariners of England*, in the lines, *Ye Gentlemen of England*, written by Martyn Parker so long before. Burns worked over the old North Country ballad of *Sir John Barleycorn*, as well as many an ancient Scottish song; and Shakespeare—but I need not multiply examples. The rude strong choruses which have sprung up in great campaigns, or at times of revolutionary excitement, have been the offspring of single minds, though verse after verse has been mated with them by the people. Such are the burdens of the French *Malbrouck* and *Ça Ira*, the Irish *Shan Van Vocht*, and our own grim battle-chorus of *John Brown's Body*—yet it would be difficult to prove that they had not " growed " like Topsy, without the formality of a beginning. I take it, in brief, that many noteworthy anonymous poems were the handiwork of single-poem makers. Artists who have become favourably known by continuous effort are not careless of their titles to successful work, nor do the book-wrights often permit specimens of the acknowledged masters to be lost.

The composers of our most familiar random poems are of several types. First, those whose one inspiration has come from a sentiment—like the love of home, of country, of sweetheart, of wife and offspring. Such have sung because a chance emotion would have vent, and their song has found a greeting in the common heart, independently of much artistic right to consideration. Next are the natural rhymesters, with their sound and fury. If one makes verses perpetually, the odds are that he will at some time find something worth to say, or that he will hit upon a theme in which his fellows have a genuine interest; and when these chances come together, the result is a popular acceptation of what is produced, while against the rest of the authors' jingles we stop our ears. Again, there are persons of high culture and beautiful thought, who have the gift of expression, but who have neglected its practice, either being sufficient unto themselves, or with their energies so diffused in other walks of life that they have only yielded in a gracious or impassioned moment to utterance of the lays for which we gratefully remember them.

A fugitive poem thus depends for its preservation upon an appeal to the universal emotions; or, through its real merits, gives pleasure to cultured minds, who ensure it ultimate renown by

Ruskin's process of the transfer of correct taste from the judicious to the unskilful. Here and there one combines these attractions, and thus achieves the high dual purpose of art. A lyric of the first kind often allies itself to an air so taking that we can hardly say whether the poetry or the music has made the hit. But some verses, like *God Save the King*, are such utter mouthing that their entire success has evidently depended on the tune. If not, old-time British loyalty was a sentiment beyond modern comprehension. Yet there are happy instances in our own language, more frequently among the Scotch and Irish dialects, of "perfect music unto noble words"; while there are other widely popular stanzas, for which musical composers have tried in vain to find a consonant melody, and thus express their very sense.

Among poems which are endeared to the people by their themes is that strictly American production, *The Bucket* of Samuel Woodworth. Without great poetical merit, it calls up simple idyllic memories to every one who has been a country boy, whether he has gained in manhood the prizes of life, or is still a trouble-tossed wanderer. To most Americans, home has been a place to start from, and only loved when left forever. Yet through the sentiment of home and a pleasant sensuous reminiscence of boyhood, *The Bucket* has found its way to numberless hearts. And Woodworth, when writing it, was lifted, for perhaps the only time in his life, to the genuine emotion of the poet, yearning after the sunny meadows, the *fons splendidior vitro*, and the moss-covered bucket of his rustic days. He was indeed a tempest-beaten fellow; a printer, born in Scituate, Mass., and a hard-worked, generally unfortunate hack and journalist, from 1816 down to his death in 1842. Except his one famous song, I can find nothing worth a day's remembrance in his collected poems, of which a volume was published in 1818, and again in 1827. Yet he wrote other pieces in the same metre and with as much care and purpose. His patriotic songs during the war of 1812 had a wide reading, as things went then. All are of the copy-book order; his was a tame, didactic mind; he never wrote but one poem, and that of itself preserves his name. *The Bucket* belongs to the lower or basic strata of the Parnassus mountain—the emotional (yet here it occurs to me that these crop out again near the apex, as in some lofty dramatic outburst, like

> Grief fills the room up of my absent child!)

and this household poem, without the factitious aid of a popular air, holds a place by its own music and the associations which it conveys.

Indeed, I am not sure that the present article was not suggested by a visit made one day to the rooms where a painter has translated into his own form of expression this and another of our simplest primary lyrics. Multitudes are now buying the pretty chromo-lithographs of Jerome Thompson's paintings of *The Old Oaken Bucket,* and *Home, Sweet Home;* nor do I hesitate to say that few more grateful and attractive pictures, within the means of the average country-dweller, can hang upon his walls, than these truthful representations of the birth-place of Samuel Woodworth, and the " Sweet Home " of John Howard Payne.

The last-named ditty, though still more obviously depending upon a sentiment, has a world of help from the air to which it was composed. Looking at the stirring life and many writings of its author, it seems strange that such ordinary stanzas should be the production by which he is known, and here mentioned as his single poem. Payne was a New Yorker, born in 1792, and, by an odd coincidence, his first essays were contributed to a juvenile paper called *The Fly,* published by Samuel Woodworth at the Boston office where the latter learned his trade. The former was only seventeen years old when he made a famous sensation at the Park, as Young Norval, following it up with the enactment of all sorts of parts at many American theatres, and soon playing as second to George Frederick Cooke. He had taken to the stage for the support of a widowed mother, breaking off a collegiate course at Union. In 1813 he went to England and came out at Drury Lane; then turned author again, and made his first literary success in the tragedy of *Brutus,* which he wrote for Edmund

Kean, and which still holds " the stage." He also wrote *Virginius* and *Therese*, and I don't know what, but the facts about *Home, Sweet Home* may bear telling again. For years Payne was an available playwright and craftsman in the London dramatic world. Whe Charles Kemble became manager of Covent Garden, he purchased a batch of our author's manuscripts for the gross sum of £230; and a play was fished out from the mess, changed by Payne into an opera, and produced as *Clari, the Maid of Milan.* Miss Tree, the elder sister of Mrs. Charles Kean, was in the first cast, and sang *Home, Sweet Home,* one of the " gems " of this piece. It made an astounding hit, was speedily the popular favourite, and even at this day we may say that the air and words are the surest key, on the reappearance of a pet *diva,* to unlock the hearts of her welcomers. Those who were present will not forget the return of Kellogg to our Academy on the 19th of last October, and the tenderness and grace with which she sang them; nor the encores of the audience, and the flowers which dropped around her till she seemed like a melodious bird in Eden. *Sweet Home* was only reckoned at £30 to its author, but was a fortune to those who purchased it. In 1832, 100,000 copies had been sold by the original publisher, and the profits within two years after its issue were two thousand guineas. For all this, it is nothing but a homely, unpoetical statement of the most characteristic sentiment of the Teutonic race. The music had gained no former triumph; but wedded to the idea of home, and sounded in Anglo-Saxon ears, it became irresistible, and will hold its own for generations. " 'Midst pleasures and palaces " is as bad as bad can be, but match it with the assertion " There's no place like Home! " and we all accept the one for the sake of the other.

Nor is it strange that in America—where homes are so transitory and people are like the brooks which go on forever—this sentiment should take hold as firmly as in the Motherland. It is because our home-tenure here *is* so precarious that we cling to its idealisation. Conversely, we have little of that itch to possess land—to own so many roods of earth to the centre—which our adopted citizens display. The Yankee undervalues the attainable, and is so used to see land at low rates about him that he can scarcely understand the eagerness with which a Frenchman or German receives his title-deeds to some barren hillside in Pennsylvania or a quarter section along the overland route.

Payne was too much of an actor to be a poet. His youthful features, judging from the likeness taken in his seventeenth year, were of a singularly mobile and expressive type. Not long ago, some of his MSS., and a portrait of him in later manhood, were offered for sale in this city, as a part of a virtuoso's collection. The face there given would readily have obtained a place in Eugene

Benson's gallery of those which are beautiful and suggestive. He was, also, too much of a playwright and author to become a great actor; and too much a man of affairs to stick to any profession continuously. As last he made a long retirement, as Consul at Tunis, and might have produced an epic if he had known how. Before this, his employments were as diverse as those of Shakespeare; but the gap between the capacities of two such beings is wide as the arch from pole to pole, though they stand on a common axis of chosen work.

As for Payne's one song, it would seem that any stanzas, thus widely known and endeared, have a more than ordinary claim for admission to a collection which aims to present the noteworthy accepted poetry of the English language. So that, while glad to repeat the general approval of Mr. Dana's volume, and to acknowledge that it contains, on the whole, the most conscientious, scholarly, and catholic presentation which has yet been made— I am surprised at the critical editor has not, in the case of *Home, Sweet Home*, so far overstepped his limit of the " truly beautiful and admirable " as to admit it. Of course it goes to the rear on the score of poetical defects; but on what ground are introduced the more objectionable stanzas of *God Save the King*? But *Home, Sweet Home* is the people's and children's song of all English-speaking countries, and its very title is a plea for a humble corner in any Household Book of Poetry.

Mention of *God Save the King* suggests national hymns, and we notice that the leading patriotic songs of France, England, and the United States, are the single works of their authors, unless we allow George Saville Carey's claim that his father wrote the British national anthem, and give credit to Queen Hortense for the words as well as the pretty music of *Partant pour la Syrie*. For Hortense, with all her faults, was a sweet musician and verse-maker, and executed other agreeable works; yet in her best-known song most exactly expressed the courtly, chivalrous vivacity of a people who fight and make love *pari passu*, and gaily interblend their patriotism, gallantry, and love of fame. Both the poem and the music have that "quality" which, refined by culture, so wins us in the minor art of France. Despite their "temporary and trivial" nature they have other claims to the affection of her people than the accident of the Second Empire. After all, they are not quite the thing, and the French Minister of War is advertising for a worthy national hymn. He will scarcely obtain it from a leading poet. Mr. Grant White has told us how national hymns are written and not written, and it is a fact that nearly all which have not grown among the people, have resulted from the glow of patriotism in the hearts of citizen-laymen, with whom love of country was a compelling inspiration.

The *Marseillaise* is a pre-eminent example of a single lyrical outburst from the soul of an unprofessional poet. It is the real battle-hymn of an oppressed France, and in her struggles for liberty will never be supplanted by any manufactured successor. After a long suppression, it was again made the national song when Louis Philippe gained the throne by the revolution of 1830; but when the Citizen-King forgot his citizenship, he, too, was compelled to flee before its chorus. It is the most historical and dramatic of lyrics. The one flight which Rouget de Lisle took was that of an eagle, soaring to the empyrean, and disdaining a lower reach. When a soldier invades the province of the poet, composes such a song at a single heat, and, like the bards of old, summons from his harp the music that shall match them, it is not safe to deny anything to the inspiration of mere amateurs. The man's whole life was crowded into that night at Strasbourg, and with it all the frenzy and devotion of a bleeding land.

Both our American national poems are the compositions of lawyers, who are known for little else which they wrote, outside the judicial reports. Neither seems to have had any sacred fury in his nature that was not evoked by patriotism. That which Judge Joseph Hopkinson gave out in *Hail, Columbia*, was of a sufficiently humdrum kind. He had the music of the *President's March* as a copy before him, and his verses are little better or worse than the air. The Judge was born in 1770, and was a spruce young lawyer in the summer of 1798, when war with France seemed imminent, and

Congress was holding an excited session at Philadelphia. He wrote his ode at a sitting, for the benefit of an actor, who had vainly exhausted the poets of the theatrical company, in an effort to adapt words to the stilted march then most in favour. Hopkinson was appealed to on Saturday, wrote the song on Sunday, heard it from a stage-box on the next evening; and it made a great sensation. The citizens joined in the chorus night after night, and the jurist-author found himself renowned for life by a rude homily upon Columbia in prose chopped to the metre. He was afterward a member of Congress, then a Judge of the United States District Court, and died within the memory of most of us at the good old age of seventy-two.

Francis Scott Key swept the chords more tunefully in his *Star-Spangled Banner*, which has merits that would give it a leasehold, independently of the spirited music to which it was composed. Its obvious rhymes and adjectives—" haughty host," " dread silence," " foul footsteps' pollution," etc., are little suited to the naturalism of our later day, but the burden,

'Tis the star-spangled banner; O long may it wave
O'er the land of the free and the home of the brave!

was that which a popular refrain should be, the strong common sentiment of a nation; and Key, for once in his life, expressed the feeling of a true poet. He died shortly after Hopkinson, whose junior he was by seven years. He wrote some religious pieces, and a few other songs, none of which have outlived their period; though one, *On the Return of Decatur*, had a brief reputation. It is in the Adams-and-Liberty metre of the *Star-Spangled Banner*, and exemplifies the sing-song rhythm into which men like Woodworth and Key are apt to fall, and which often commends itself to the popular taste. It is the bacon-and-greens, so to speak, of the feast of song, and not much relished by cultivated palates.

That most original and resonant lyric, the *Carmen Bellicosum* of Guy Humphrey McMaster, is far removed from these, except by the common theme of defence of country. Here is a noble chant indeed! Trumbull, in his pictures, effected no more than this writer has given us with a single dash of the pen—an interpretation of the very spirit of '76. The *Carmen Bellicosum*—every one will recall its opening verse,

> In their ragged regimentals
> Stood the old Continentals,
>   Yielding not—

occupies a unique position among English lyrics. There is nothing like it in our language; 'tis the ringing, characteristic utterance of an original man. There is a perfect wedding of sense to sound, and of both to the spirit of the theme. To include a picture often ruins a song; but here we have the knot of patriots clustered upon a battle-hillside,

the powder cracking amain, the old-fashioned
colonel galloping with drawn sword, and as

> Rounder, rounder, rounder, roars the old six-pounder,
>   Hurling death,

it seems a heavier piece of ordnance, and charged
with weightier issues, than the whole park of
artillery in a modern armament.

The song will last with the memory of revolutionary days. I know little of its author, save that
he is also a lawyer and a judge, presiding over the
Steuben County Court in this, his native State. He
is now about forty years of age, and must have
been quite young when his *Carmen* appeared in
the old *Knickerbocker Magazine*. If a stripling
attorney will enter the minstrel lists, sound such
a potent blast, then withdraw himself to the happy
life of a country-gentleman, nor be heard again
through all these years, he also must, for the
present, be numbered in our catalogue of the
single-poem poets.

McMaster is a Scotch or North-Irish patronymic,
and the Scotch have ever been in the custom of
producing fugitive lyrics of a true poetical quality.
These ditties relate more frequently to the strongest
of all emotions—that of love between man and
woman—than to the love of home or fatherland.
Two of the sweetest will at once recur to the reader.
Auld Robin Gray was composed by Anne Lindsay,
afterward Lady Barnard, as long ago as 1772, at
Balcarras in Fife. Her father was the Earl of that

ilk. She was an elegant, spirited girl, not yet out of her teens, when an old air, set to a loose old song, *The Bridegroom grat when the Sun gaed doun,* gave her a motive for her work. The lassie had learned the tune, in such mischievous ways as our liberal maids doubtless know of in these prudish times, and thought the pensive measure deserved more fitting words. She chose for her text the world-wide plaint that " Crabbed Age and Youth cannot live together "—a theme as ancient in English as Chaucer's *January and May*—took the name of Gray from an old herd in the vicinage, and wrote as sweet and pathetic a ballad as exists in any tongue. The first stanza,

When the sheep are in the fauld and the kye at hame,

is now, I believe, the only one sung to the antique tune. From the second, " Young Jamie lov'd me weel," to the close, the music, written thirty years since by the Rev. W. Lewes, is still most in use. Lady Anne's ballad was not given to the public till 1776, and, as it at once became famous, a prolonged dispute arose concerning its authorship. Modesty prevented the authoress from claiming her laurels. How could a debonair young maiden own herself familiar with the wanton ditty, *The Bridegroom Grat*? Not till she had been many years the wedded wife of Sir Andrew Barnard, and the shadows of death were close at hand, did she write her letter to Sir Walter, avowing the authorship, and narrating at length what I have briefly told. She composed a few other verses, but nothing to compare with the ballad for which we remember her name.

There is pretty good warrant for saying that the soldiers' darling, *Annie Laurie*, was the work of Mr. Douglas, of Fingland, who courted Anne, a fair daughter of Sir Robert Laurie, the first baronet of Maxwelton. This was near the commencement of the last century. The song, as it now exists, is generally classed as anonymous in our anthologies; but has been so refined and annealed through various crucibles that the current version is quite different from the two stanzas which Douglas wrote, and certainly more artistic. His are thus given in the *Ballad Book*, which contains the earliest printed copy:

> Maxwelton banks are bonnie
>   Where early fa's the dew;
> Where I and Annie Laurie
>   Made up the promise true;
> Made up the promise true,
>   And never forget will I,
> And for bonnie Annie Laurie
>   I'd lay me doun and die.

> She's backit like a peacock,
>   She's breistit like a swan,
> She's jimp about the middle,
>   Her waist you weel micht span;
> Her waist you weel micht span;
>   And she has a rolling eye,
> And for bonnie Annie Laurie
>   I'd lay me doun and die.

The heroine's rolling eye cast its glances away

from poor Douglas, and she married a Mr. Ferguson, of Craigdarrock, who found some better mode of winning a maiden's heart than singing under her window-panes. After all, the pleasure is as great in loving as in being loved; and, to put the matter allegorically, Apollo, indignant at the slight inflicted by Venus upon his servant, gave him, unawares, a seat in his temple, and ordained that, for centuries, lovers should sing the song of him who sang in vain.

What manlier love-poetry was ever written than the verses, *To his Mistress*, of James Grahame, Marquis of Montrose, wherein he vowed

> I'll make thee famous by my pen,
> And glorious by my sword!

The poem itself fulfilled half the pledge. More than two hundred years have gone by, and still no lines are more often quoted than this quatrain from the same lyric:

> He either fears his fate too much,
> Or his deserts are small,
> Who dares not put it to the touch
> To gain or lose it all.

Not more famous is the distich,

> Stone walls do not a prison make,
> Nor iron bars a cage,

from Dick Lovelace's stanzas *To Althea, from Prison*; though the handsome cavalier left many another ditty to distinguish him from our birds of a single flight. The lines here mentioned are the second example we have reached of the music, real or imagined, of imprisoned songsters; and to them I might add the Latin verses, *In Dura Catena*, attributed to the Queen of Scots—certainly the one poem written by the Fayre Gospeller, Anne Askewe, who was burned at the stake by command of brutal and dying Harry, in 1546. After her last examination upon the rack, she was inspired to utter, in a Newgate cell, the heroic defiance:

> Like as the arméd knight
>   Appointed to the field,
> With this world will I fight,
>   And faith shall be my shield.

We can well believe the statement of one who saw the girl led to execution, that " she had an angel's countenance and a smiling face." Poor Anne's verses have been preserved rather for her story's sake and for their religious ardour, than for poetical excellence; and it is noticeable that hymns, and fugitive lyrics animated with religious hope or aspiration, have a fairer chance, other things being equal, of obtaining a continued hearing than almost any class—those appealing to the " master passion " alone excepted. Reflective poems, tinged with that melancholy which comes to one chastened by the experiences of life, are also widely in favour.

I would not live alway has everywhere made the name of our venerable citizen, Dr. Muhlenberg, a household word. He wrote it many years since, with no thought that it would ever be used for the devotions of the church, but has long seen it in the hymnology of most Protestant denominations, and encountered many pseudo-claimants to its authorship. Among these I knew an old printer, of Litchfield, Connecticut, who imagined he had composed it, and periodically filled a column in the village newspaper with evidence to further his claim. But Dr. Muhlenberg's title cannot be shaken. Another poem, upon a kindred theme, though with the element of hope omitted, was popular with the sad Calvinists of the last generation, but had almost faded out, when an accidental connection with the name of President Lincoln gave it a new lease of life, which may continue with the memory of the great Liberator. He was so fond of repeating the monody,

O why should the spirit of mortal be proud?

that by some persons he was credited with its composition, until the Press recognised the work of William Knox, who died A.D. 1825, at Edinburgh, in his thirty-seventh year. These lines are expressive of a brooding Scotch melancholy, pitched in a minor religious key, and in certain moods not ineffective as a quaint and forceful meditation upon an ever-pressing theme. Their whole motive is condensed in the terse old formula, "All flesh is grass"; but a Sicilian poet, the pagan Moschus, found even this an insufficient image of the hopelessness of mortality. Let me give a naked translation (from the wonderful *Epitaph of Bion*) of the most sorrowful passage ever constructed outside of Hebrew writ:

Even the mallows—alas! alas!—when once in the garden
They, or the pale-green parsley and crisp-growing anise,
    have perished,
Afterward they will live and flourish again at their season;

We, the great and brave, or the wise—when death has
    benumbed us—
Deaf in the hollow ground a silent, infinite slumber
Sleep; forever we lie in the trance that knoweth no waking.

The drear and homely verses of Mr. Lincoln's favourite poem have already gained the suffrage of those gentlemen whose favour is such an omen of longevity—the makers of school-books. I find it in the latest *Reader*, along with such selections as Lincoln's *Address at Gettysburg*, Read's *Sheridan's Ride*, Bayard Taylor's *Scott and the Veteran*, Whittier's *Barbara Fritchie*, and other new-born pieces, which are to the rising generation what the *Speech of Patrick Henry*, *Marco Bozzaris*, or *Stand! The Ground's your Own, my Braves!* were to ourselves, a few—it seems a *very* few—summers and winters ago.

Sexagenarians can remember the notoriety given Herbert Knowles—an English youth who died at Canterbury in his twentieth year—by Robert Southey, who set him forth in the *London Quarterly* as a second Kirke White. Knowles was a precocious religious poet, and his surviving verses are *Lines Written in the Churchyard of Richmond*, to the text, Matt. xvii. 4:

> Methinks it is good to be here!
> If thou wilt, let us build, but to whom?

These will appear in many future compilations; and so will the thoughtful numbers of our own countrywoman, Harriet Winslow:

> Why thus longing, thus forever sighing
> For the far-off, unattained and dim?

But a more impassioned and elevated single poem is that fervent composition imagined to have been written by *Milton on his Blindness*—the work of a Quaker lady, Elizabeth Lloyd,[1] of Philadelphia. These truly " noble numbers " deserve the attention which they gained upon their first appearance, at which time paragraphists went so far as to call them Milton's own, and credit them to an Oxford edition of his poems. They are not Miltonic in the least, but exhibit a rapturous inspiration, and of themselves have insured their writer a long regard.

Occasionally straightforward rhymes, with a moral, like *The Three Warnings*, of Mrs. Hester Lynch Piozzi—Johnson's Mrs. Thrale—have held their own, either for their shrewd wisdom, or for the associations connected with their author.

But which of all the asteroids that have passed before our vision—whether tinged with a domestic, patriotic, amorous, or sombre light—will be longer

---

[1] Now Mrs. E. L. Howell.

or more lovingly regarded than the children's own poem and dearest—'*Twas the Night before Christmas*? written for them so daintily by a sage college professor, Clement C. Moore, to wit, long time a resident of this old Dutch city, and deceased (peace to his ashes!) hardly more than four or five years ago. *A Visit from St. Nicholas* is dear to the little ones for its exquisite fancies and the annual legend, and to us all for our beautiful memories of childhood and home. It is linked with the natal festival of Christendom, is entirely true to its purpose, and finished as deftly as if the author had been a professional poet. Few of those who were his contemporaries, and who know every word of this sparkling fantasia, have been familiar with the details of his quiet and industrious life. He was born in 1779, and grew up a studious philologist, as his Hebrew and English lexicon, issued in 1809, still attests. Twelve years afterward he was made Professor of Biblical Learning in the New York Episcopal Theological Seminary, and more lately took the chair of Oriental and Greek Literature. Despite all this, and rich besides, he wrote poetry, and a volume of his rhymes appeared in 1844. They were of an ephemeral nature, except the poem which I would have gone far to hear him repeat in his old, old age, and for which my younger readers must always remember his venerable name.

Let us not overlook a lyric, of which many have, probably, already thought — the Rev. Charles Wolfe's *Burial of Sir John Moore*. No fugitive piece has had a wider or more potential circulation than this school-boy favourite; yet who, besides the men of letters, have troubled themselves concerning its author, or known of other graceful verses by his hand? A few have read the song which he made to the Irish air, *Grammachree*. It is said that he sang the music over until it affected him to tears, and impelled him to write his equally pathetic lament, in such stanzas as the following:

> If I had thought thou couldst have died
> I might not weep for thee;
> But I forgot when by thy side,
> That thou couldst mortal be.
> It never through my mind had past
> The time would e'er be o'er,
> And I on thee should look my last,
> And thou shouldst smile no more!

But we must here cease our observation of poets who come strictly within the prescribed limits of the telescopic field. I have barely space enough for reference to a few of those whose reputation has been won by life-long devotion to their art, yet of whose respective productions some one piece has, in each instance, gained the world's ear, and often to the neglect of other excellent works. The poems hitherto considered are more widely known than their authors; while to name a poet of the class to which I now allude, is to start in the mind the key-measure of his representative poem. Examples of this effect are always numerous, and especially in present re-

membrance of the poets who wrote long ago—
Time so winnows out and sets apart the general
choice, whether it be such coarse healthful grain
as that from which jovial Bishop Still brewed his
Good Ale:

> Back and side go bare, go bare;
> Both foot and hand go cold;
> But belly, God send thee good ale enow,
> Whether be it new or old!

or the golden barley on which singing birds like
Thomas Lodge and Sir Henry Wotton had fed, ere
they warbled such dainty lyrics as *Love in my
Bosom like a Bee*, and *You Meaner Beauties of the
Night*. These two, and many another canticle of
their period, you can find in R. H. Stoddard's
most choice selection of English *Melodies and
Madrigals*. Are James Shirley and Edmund Waller
popularly remembered by single lyrics? Nearly
so, for in the one case the two stanzas of Shirley's
Victorious Men of Earth, with the alteration of a
couplet, would be in the stately measures of that
grandest and most solemn of our minor poesies,
Death's Final Conquest:

> The glories of our birth and state
> Are shadows, not substantial things;

while the feeling and theme of the two lyrics are
alike, and, though each is perfect in itself, they
read like portions of a divided poem. And Waller's
name is still popularly connected with *Go, Lovely
Rose*, and *On a Girdle*, out of the whole mass of

his songs, epistles, epitaphs, and panegyrics, though Professor Lowell, in his delightful citation of Dryden, and perhaps animated by that scorn of Waller's truckling which every true and noble poet must feel, says that the latter has lived mainly on the credit of a single couplet in the lines closing his *Divine Poesy*.

The late English period, however, is all that I can glance at. To mention John Logan is to revive the *Ode to the Cuckoo*, yet 'tis by no means certain that Logan did not refine this standard poem from the crude metal left by his friend Michael Bruce. His song on a wild old theme, touched by so many melodists, *The Dowie Dens of Yarrow*, deserves as long a reputation; though of all the Yarrow ballads, that by William Hamilton, *Busk ye, Busk ye, my Bonnie, Bonnie Bride!* is the nonpareil. Every one has been affected by the simplicity, music, and exquisite pathos of Caroline Oliphant, the Baroness Nairn's *Land o' the Leal*:

> I'm wearin' awa', John,
> Like snow-wreaths in thaw, John;
> I'm wearin' awa'
>   To the land o' the leal.

The author died in 1845, at the ripe age of eighty years, and throughout her life wrote poetry, some of it humorous, which was quite the fashion in Scotland. *The Laird o' Cockpen* had a wide reading, and is excellent of its kind. There was Susanna Blamire, the "Muse of Cumberland," who made sweet use of the border dialect in her ballads and songs. *The Siller Crown* is always associated with her name:

> And ye sall walk in silk attire,
>   And siller hae to spare,
> Gin ye'll consent to be his bride
>   Nor think o' Donald mair.

There, also, is Sheridan's granddaughter, Lady Dufferin, who has composed very many lyrics, but is known by her most beautiful ballad, *The Irish Emigrant's Lament*, sometimes wrongly credited to her sister, Mrs. Norton. The words of *I'm sitting on the Stile, Mary!* and the genuine melody to which they are sung, have that about them which will last. Did Dennis Florence M'Carthy or John Francis Waller write *Dance light, for my Heart lies under your Feet, Love*? I should like to know, for equal authorities ascribe it to one and the other, and it is too graceful an Irish ballad to go a-begging; 'tis almost as good as the song of Irish songs, Allingham's *Lovely Mary Donnelly*. Of Thomas Noel's *Rhymes and Roundelays*, published in London, 1841, the poem all know is a strange and grotesque lyric, *The Pauper's Drive*, with its dreary burden:

> Rattle his bones over the stones!
> He's only a pauper, whom nobody owns.

Perhaps *Give me the Old*, written by R. H. Messenger, a Bostonian, from the theme "Old wine to drink," etc., should have been included with the class first under review. The New

Yorker, James Aldrich, made verses innumerable,
but we only speak of two little stanzas, entitled
A Death Bed, so curiously like and unlike Hood's
We watched her breathing through the Night.
The names of three poets—and on whom in the
South have fallen their mantles?—quickly bring
to mind three songs which won them most lovers;
remembering the scholar, poet, and enthusiast,
Richard Henry Wilde, one finds himself murmur-
ing that soft perfection, *My Life is like the Summer
Rose*; next comes Edward C. Pinkney's chivalrous
Health : "I drink this cup to one made up of
loveliness alone!" and with mention of Philip
Pendleton Cooke, all think of *Florence Vane*,
which, however, is a close study after E. A. Poe.
The latter is himself constantly entitled the author
of *The Raven*, yet, for true poetical qualities, his
Annabel Lee, Haunted Palace, The City in the Sea,
and that remarkable dithyrambic fantasy, *The
Bells*, are more valued by the selectest taste. Why
does every one speak of the late General Morris as
the writer of *Woodman, Spare that Tree*? Because
this lyric, almost as widely known as *Sweet Home*,
has the simple elements of a song proper, and in
this respect might not have been so good if the
author had been a greater poet. I think it deserves
a corner, opposite the other, in any liberal collection of our songs. Hoffman's *Sparkling and Bright*
had a like trick of catching the public ear. The
Rev. Ralph Hoyt, who once published a volume
of quaint and original poems, is known as the

author of *Old*, and he has been so long silent that it is not wholly my fault if he is not reckoned with the list of contemporaries. Two fugitive lyrics, now in my mind, may belong rather to the classification first made, though why I should here select them, I can hardly tell. One is *The Voice of the Grass*,

Here I come creeping, creeping everywhere!

by Sarah Roberts, of New Hampshire. The other —who is it by?—*In Summer when the Days were long*. Each was composed by a true poet, and is an addition to literature in its unpretending way.

But to return for a moment to our main purpose. The fortunate single-poems, before mentioned, were either the spirited efforts of amateurs, or the sole hits achieved by the Quinces and Triplets of their day. If a person of culture has made, with easy hand, a chance success; or, if patient dullards woo our gracious Thea until they flatter her into a smile of favour, or steal upon an unguarded moment to catch certain echoes of her voice; all this is nothing in behalf of amateur art—nor are they to be placed on a level with the consecrated poets. For the latter can, with certainty, again and again, excel the random work of those who come not in by the appointed door. A large proportion of the minor art of our most approved poets is made up of pieces, each of which, if the only specimen of its author, might have received

preservation as an attractive fugitive poem. We
need not mention the great names of the past; but
can any doubt that such would be the case with
Browning's *Evelyn Hope*, and *How they Brought
the Good News from Ghent to Aix*; with Tennyson's
Bugle Song and *Come into the Garden, Maud*;
with Longfellow's *Excelsior*; Lowell's *The Courtin'*,
and *To a Dandelion*; Bryant's *The Battle-Field*;
with those exquisite quatrains by Aldrich, *Ah,
sad are they who know not Love!* with Boker's
Dirge for Phil Kearny, Winter's beautiful
lyric, *Love's Queen*, Taylor's *Bedouin Song*, and
Daughter of Egypt; with Swinburne's *If Love were
what the Rose is*; or, indeed, with scores of other
imaginative and finished specimens of these and
other master-hands? For I have mentioned the
foregoing at merest hap-hazard, as minor productions likely, from one cause or another, to have
become endeared to the people or the critical
few, and each for itself to have preserved an
author's name.

Hereafter, more than ever, there will be no royal
road to the honours of the poet. It is necessary, in
this period, that every cabinet picture or sketch
should show the hand of the master, and be a gem
of its kind. More is required to make good work
distinctive. High technical finish is so well understood, that it is again asked of the poet, not only
that he shall have the art of sweet-saying, but
that he shall have something to say. Mrs. Browning
sings of the great Pan, down among the river reeds,

"making a poet out of a man"; but often I wish some power would make *men* out of plenty of the modern poets. A painter has to look through the Old World for his masterpieces, and to sit long at the feet of his elders for the secrets of colour and form; but the versifier's greatest models are at hand in every village library, and the contagion which the press brings to our doors constantly leads hundreds to mistake inclination for power, or an imitative knowledge of the *technique* of poetry for a true inspiration. They catch the knack of making such verses as only genius could have invented fifty years ago, and which then might justly have won them laurels.

Thus no art is so easy as that of poetry; but in none is it so difficult to achieve a distinctive individuality. It is the lowest and highest of arts. In it, more than in any other, amateur work is to be discouraged, as most easily essayed, and as fostering dilettanteism and corrupt taste. There is little danger of sending away angels unawares. I was in the studio of a wise and famous painter, who has learned the secrets of the dawn, when a young aspirant came with a specimen of his work, and sought counsel as to his adoption of the painter's art as a calling for life. My friend looked at the sketch, kindly talked with the youth of a painter's struggles and self-denials, and of the tide constantly pressing the finest genius back from its goal, and so sent his listener away with few words of encouragement or hope. "Now," said I, "you know that boy's picture had merit; why did you treat him so harshly?" He answered, "If he has the right stuff in him, this will make no difference; he will paint on, though the ghost of Raphael should warn him to give way; and will succeed in his art. If he has not, I am doing him the highest benefit by keeping from him that 'crown of sorrow' which is inevitable for one who has not clearly discerned the true purpose of his life."

FALSTAFF [1]

By George Radford

There is more material for a life of Falstaff than for a life of Shakespeare, though for both there is a lamentable dearth. The difficulties of the biographer are, however, different in the two cases. There is nothing, or next to nothing, in Shakespeare's works which throws light on his own story; and such evidence as we have is of the kind called circumstantial. But Falstaff constantly gives us reminiscences or allusions to his earlier life, and his companions also tell us stories which ought to help us in a biography. The evidence, such as it is, is direct; and the only inference we have to draw is that from the statement to the truth of the statement.

It has been justly remarked by Sir James Stephen, that this very inference is perhaps the most difficult one of all to draw correctly. The inference from so-called circumstantial evidence, if you have enough of it, is much surer; for whilst facts cannot lie, witnesses can, and frequently do.

[1] From *Obiter Dicta*. The one essay contributed by another hand to Mr. Birrell's delightful volume.

The witnesses on whom we have to rely for the facts are Falstaff and his companions—especially Falstaff.

When an old man tries to tell you the story of his youth, he sees the facts through a distorting subjective medium, and gives an impression of his history and exploits more or less at variance with the bare facts as seen by a contemporary outsider. The scientific Goethe, though truthful enough in the main, certainly fails in his reminiscences to tell a plain unvarnished tale. And Falstaff was *not* habitually truthful. Indeed, that Western American, who wrote affectionately on the tomb of a comrade, " As a truth-crusher he was unrivalled," had probably not given sufficient attention to Falstaff's claims in this matter. Then Falstaff's companions are not witnesses above suspicion. Generally speaking, they lie open to the charge made by P. P. against the wags of his parish, that they were men delighting more in their own conceits than in the truth. These are some of our difficulties, and we ask the reader's indulgence in our endeavours to overcome them. We will tell the story from our hero's birth, and will not begin longer *before* that event than is usual with biographers.

The question, *Where* was Falstaff born ? has given us some trouble. We confess to having once entertained a strong opinion that he was a Devonshire man. This opinion was based simply on the flow and fertility of his wit as shown in his conversation, and the rapid and fantastic play of his imagination. But we sought in vain for any verbal provincialisms in support of this theory, and there was something in the character of the man that rather went against it. Still, we clung to the opinion, till we found that philology was against us, and that the Falstaffs unquestionably came from Norfolk.

The name is of Scandinavian origin; and we find in *Domesday* that a certain Falstaff held freely from the king a church at Stamford. These facts are of great importance. The thirst for which Falstaff was always conspicuous was no doubt inherited—was, in fact, a Scandinavian thirst. The pirates of early English times drank as well as they fought, and their descendants who invade England—now that the war of commerce has superseded the war of conquest—still bring the old thirst with them, as any one can testify who has enjoyed the hospitality of the London Scandinavian Club. Then this church was no doubt a familiar landmark in the family; and when Falstaff stated, late in life, that if he hadn't forgotten what the inside of a church was like, he was a peppercorn and a brewer's horse, he was thinking with some remorse of the family temple.

Of the family between the Conquest and Falstaff's birth we know nothing, except that, according to Falstaff's statement, he had a grandfather who left him a seal ring worth forty marks. From this statement we might infer that the ring was an heirloom, and consequently that Falstaff was an eldest son, and the head of his family. But we must be careful in drawing our inferences, for Prince Henry frequently told Falstaff that the ring was copper; and on one occasion, when Falstaff alleged that his pocket had been picked at the *Boar's Head*, and this seal-ring and three or four bonds of forty pounds apiece abstracted, the Prince assessed the total loss at eightpence.

After giving careful attention to the evidence, and particularly to the conduct of Falstaff on the occasion of the alleged robbery, we come to the conclusion that the ring *was* copper, and was not an heirloom. This leaves us without any information about Falstaff's family prior to his birth. He was born (as he himself informs the Lord Chief Justice) about three o'clock in the afternoon, with a white head and something a round belly. Falstaff's corpulence, therefore, as well as his thirst, was congenital. Let those who are not born with his comfortable figure sigh in vain to attain his stately proportions. This is a thing which Nature gives us at our birth as much as the Scandinavian thirst or the shaping spirit of imagination.

Born somewhere in Norfolk, Falstaff's early months and years were no doubt rich with the promise of his after greatness. We have no record of his infancy, and are tempted to supply the gap with Rabelais' chapters on Gargantua's babyhood. But regard for the truth compels us to add nothing

that cannot fairly be deduced from the evidence.
We leave the strapping boy in his swaddling-clothes
to answer the question *when* he was born. Now, it
is to be regretted that Falstaff, who was so precise
about the hour of his birth, should not have mentioned the year. On this point we are again left
to inference from conflicting statements. We have
this distinct point to start from—that Falstaff, in
or about the year 1401, gives his age as some fifty
or by'r Lady inclining to three-score. It is true
that in other places he represents himself as old,
and again in another states that he and his accom-
plices in the Gadshill robbery are in the vaward of
their youth. The Chief Justice reproves him for
this affectation of youth, and puts a question
(which, it is true, elicits no admission from Falstaff)
as to whether every part of him is not blasted
with antiquity.

We are inclined to think that Falstaff rather
understated his age when he described himself as
by'r Lady inclining to three-score, and that we
shall not be far wrong if we set down 1340 as the
year of his birth. We cannot be certain to a year
or two. There is a similar uncertainty about the
year of Sir Richard Whittington's birth. But both
these great men, whose careers afford in some
respects striking contrasts, were born within a few
years of the middle of the fourteenth century.

Falstaff's childhood was no doubt spent in
Norfolk; and we learn from his own lips that he
plucked geese, played truant, and whipped top,

and that he did not escape beating. That he had
brothers and sisters we know; for he tells us that
he is *John* with them and *Sir John* with all Europe.
We do not know the dame or pedant who taught
his young idea how to shoot and formed his
manners; but Falstaff says that *if* his manners
became him not, he was a fool that taught them
him. This does not throw much light on his early
education: for it is not clear that the remark
applies to that period, and in any case it is purely
hypothetical.

But Falstaff, like so many boys since his time,
left his home in the country and came to London.
His brothers and sisters he left behind him, and
we hear no more of them. Probably none of them
ever attained eminence, as there is no record of
Falstaff's having attempted to borrow money of
them. We know Falstaff so well as a tun of a man,
a horse-back-breaker, and so forth, that it is not
easy to form an idea of what he was in his youth.
But if we trace back the sack-stained current of
his life to the day when, full of wonder and hope,
he first rode into London, we shall find him as
different from Shakespeare's picture of him as the
Thames at Iffley is from the Thames at London
Bridge. His figure was shapely; he had no difficulty *then* in seeing his own knee, and if he was
not able, as he afterwards asserted, to creep
through an alderman's ring, nevertheless he had
all the grace and activity of youth. He was just
such a lad (to take a description almost contem-

porary) as the Squier who rode with the Canterbury
Pilgrims:

> A lover and a lusty bacheler,
> With lockes crull as they were laid in presse,
> Of twenty yere of age he was, I gesse.
> Of his stature he was of even lengthe,
> And wonderly deliver, and grete of strengthe.
>
> .   .   .   .   .   .
>
> Embrouded was he, as it were a mede,
> All ful of freshe floures, white and rede;
> Singing he was, or floyting alle the day,
> He was as freshe as is the moneth of May.
> Short was his goune, with sleves long and wide,
> Wel coude he sitte on hors, and fayre ride,
> He coulde songes make, and wel endite,
> Just and eke dance, and wel pourtraie and write.
> So hot he loved, that by nightertale
> He slep no more than doth the nightingale.

Such was Falstaff at the age of twenty, or
something earlier, when he entered at Clement's
Inn, where were many other young men reading
law, and preparing for their call to the Bar. How
much law he read it is impossible now to ascertain. That he had, in later life, a considerable
knowledge of the subject is clear, but this may
have been acquired like Mr. Micawber's, by experience, as defendant on civil process. We are
inclined to think he read but little. *Amici fures
temporis:* and he had many friends at Clement's
Inn who were not smugs, nor, indeed, reading men
in any sense. There was John Doit of Staffordshire,
and Black George Barnes, and Francis Pickbone,
and Will Squele, a Cotswold man, and Robert

Shallow from Gloucestershire. Four of these were such swingebucklers as were not to be found again in all the Inns o' Court, and we have it on the authority of Justice Shallow that Falstaff was a good backswordsman, and that before he had done growing he broke the head of Skogan at the Court gate. This Skogan appears to have been Court-jester to Edward III. No doubt the natural rivalry between the amateur and the professional caused the quarrel, and Skogan must have been a good man if he escaped with a broken head only, and without damage to his reputation as a professional wit. The same day that Falstaff did this deed of daring—the only one of the kind recorded of him—Shallow fought with Sampson Stockfish, a fruiterer, behind Gray's Inn. Shallow was a gay dog in his youth, according to his own account: he was called Mad Shallow, Lusty Shallow—indeed, he was called anything. He played Sir Dagonet in Arthur's show at Mile End Green; and no doubt Falstaff and the rest of the set were cast for other parts in the same pageant. These tall fellows of Clement's Inn kept well together, for they liked each other's company, and they needed each other's help in a row in Turnbull Street or elsewhere. Their watchword was " Hem, boys! " and they made the old Strand ring with their songs as they strolled home to their chambers of an evening. They heard the chimes at midnight—which, it must be confessed, does not seem to us a desperately dissipated entertainment. But midnight was a late hour in those days. The paralytic masher of the present day, who is most alive at midnight, rises at noon. *Then* the day began earlier with a long morning, followed by a pleasant period called the forenoon. Under modern conditions we spend the morning in bed, and to palliate our sloth call the forenoon and most of the rest of the day, the morning. These young men of Clement's Inn were a lively, not to say a rowdy, set. They would do anything that led to mirth or mischief. What passed when they lay all night in the wind-mill in St. George's Field we do not quite know; but we are safe in assuming that they did not go there to pursue their legal duties, or to grind corn. Anyhow, forty years after, that night raised pleasant memories.

John Falstaff was the life and centre of this set, as Robert Shallow was the butt of it. The latter had few personal attractions. According to Falstaff's portrait of him, he looked like a man made after supper of a cheese-paring. When he was naked he was for all the world like a forked radish, with a head fantastically carved upon it with a knife: he was so forlorn that his dimensions to any thick sight were invincible: he was the very genius of famine; and a certain section of his friends called him mandrake: he came ever in the rearward of the fashion, and sung those tunes to the over-scutched huswives that he heard the car-men whistle, and sware they were his fancies or his good-nights. Then he had the honour of having his head burst by John o' Gaunt, for crowding

among the Marshal's men in the Tilt-yard, and
this was matter for continual gibe from Falstaff
and the other boys. Falstaff was in the van of the
fashion, was witty himself without being at that
time the cause that wit was in others. No one
could come within range of his wit without being
attracted and overpowered. Late in life Falstaff
deplores nothing so much in the character of
Prince John of Lancaster as this, that a man
cannot make him laugh. He felt this defect in the
Prince's character keenly, for laughter was Falstaff's familiar spirit, which never failed to come
at his call. It was by laughter that young Falstaff
fascinated his friends and ruled over them. There
are only left to us a few scraps of his conversation,
and these have been, and will be to all time, the
delight of all good men. The Clement's Inn boys
who enjoyed the feast, of which we have but the
crumbs left to us, were happy almost beyond the
lot of man. For there is more in laughter than is
allowed by the austere, or generally recognised by
the jovial. By laughter man is distinguished from
the beasts, but the cares and sorrows of life have
all but deprived man of this distinguishing grace,
and degraded him to a brutal solemnity. Then
comes (alas, how rarely!) a genius such as Falstaff's,
which restores the power of laughter and transforms
the stolid brute into man. This genius approaches
nearly to the divine power of creation, and we may
truly say, "Some for less were deified." It is no
marvel that young Falstaff's friends assiduously

served the deity who gave them this good gift. At
first he was satisfied with the mere exercise of his
genial power, but he afterwards made it service-
able to him. It was but just that he should receive
tribute from those who were beholden to him, for
a pleasure which no other could confer.

It was now that Falstaff began to recognise what
a precious gift was his congenital Scandinavian
thirst, and to lose no opportunity of gratifying it.
We have his mature views on education, and we
may take them as an example of the general truth
that old men habitually advise a young one to
shape the conduct of his life after their own.
Rightly to apprehend the virtues of sherris-sack
is the first qualification in an instructor of youth.
"If I had a thousand sons," says he, "the first
humane principles I would teach them should be
to forswear thin potations, and to addict themselves to sack"; and further: "There's never
none of these demure boys come to any proof;
for their drink doth so over-cool their blood, and
making many fish-meals, that they fall into a kind
of male green sickness; and then when they marry
they get wenches: they are generally fools and
cowards, which some of us should be too but for
inflammation." There can be no doubt that
Falstaff did not in early life over-cool his blood,
but addicted himself to sack, and gave the subject
a great part of his attention for all the remainder
of his days.

It may be that he found the subject too absorbing to allow of his giving much attention to old Father Antic the Law. At any rate, he was never called to the Bar, and posterity cannot be too thankful that his great mind was not lost in " the abyss of legal eminence " which has received so many men who might have adorned their country. That he was fitted for a brilliant legal career can admit of no doubt. His power of detecting analogies in cases apparently different, his triumphant handling of cases apparently hopeless, his wonderful readiness in reply, and his dramatic instinct, would have made him a powerful advocate. It may have been owing to difficulties with the Benchers of the period over questions of discipline, or it may have been a distaste for the profession itself, which induced him to throw up the law and adopt the profession of arms.

We know that while he was still at Clement's Inn he was page to Lord Thomas Mowbray, who was afterwards created Earl of Nottingham and Duke of Norfolk. It must be admitted that here (as elsewhere in Shakespeare) there is some little chronological difficulty. We will not inquire too curiously, but simply accept the testimony of Justice Shallow on the point. Mowbray was an able and ambitious lord, and Falstaff, as page to him, began his military career with every advantage. The French wars of the later years of Edward III. gave frequent and abundant opportunity for distinction. Mowbray distinguished himself in Court and in camp, and we should like to believe that Falstaff was in the sea-fight when Mowbray defeated the French fleet and captured vast quantities of sack from the enemy. Unfortunately, there is no record whatever of Falstaff's early military career, and beyond his own ejaculation, " Would to God that my name was not so terrible to the enemy as it is! " and the (possible) inference from it that he must have made his name terrible in some way, we have no evidence that he was ever in the field before the battle of Shrewsbury. Indeed, the absence of evidence on this matter goes strongly to prove the negative. Falstaff boasts of his valour, his alacrity, and other qualities which were not apparent to the casual observer, but he never boasts of his services in battle. If there had been anything of the kind to which he could refer with complacency, there is no moral doubt that he would have mentioned it freely, adding such embellishments and circumstances as he well knew how.

In the absence of evidence as to the course of life, we are left to conjecture how he spent the forty years, more or less, between the time of his studies at Clement's Inn and the day when Shakespeare introduces him to us. We have no doubt that he spent all, or nearly all, this time in London. His habits were such as are formed by life in a great city: his conversation betrays a man who has lived, as it were, in a crowd, and the busy haunts of men were the appropriate scene for the display of his great qualities. London, even then, was a

great city, and the study of it might well absorb
a lifetime. Falstaff knew it well, from the Court,
with which he always preserved a connexion, to
the numerous taverns where he met his friends and
eluded his creditors. The *Boar's Head* in East-
cheap was his headquarters, and, like Barnabee's,
two centuries later, his journeys were from tavern
to tavern; and, like Barnabee, he might say
" Multum bibi, nunquam pransi." To begin with,
no doubt the dinner bore a fair proportion to the
fluid which accompanied it, but by degrees the
liquor encroached on and superseded the viands,
until his tavern bills took the shape of the one
purloined by Prince Henry, in which there was
but one halfpennyworth of bread to an intolerable
deal of sack. It was this inordinate consumption
of sack (and not sighing and grief, as he suggests)
which blew him up like a bladder. A life of leisure
in London always had, and still has, its tempta-
tions. Falstaff's means were described by the
Chief Justice of Henry IV. as very slender, but
this was after they had been wasted for years.
Originally they were more ample, and gave him
the opportunity of living at ease with his friends.
No domestic cares disturbed the even tenor of his
life. Bardolph says he was better accommodated
than with a wife. Like many another man about
town, he thought about settling down when he
was getting up in years. He weekly swore, so he
tells us, to marry old Mistress Ursula, but this
was only after he saw the first white hair on his

chin. But he never led Mistress Ursula to the altar. The only other women for whom he formed an early attachment were Mistress Quickly, the hostess of the *Boar's Head*, and Doll Tearsheet, who is described by the page as a proper gentlewoman, and a kinswoman of his master's. There is no denying that Falstaff was on terms of intimacy with Mistress Quickly, but he never admitted that he made her an offer of marriage. She, however, asserted it in the strongest terms and with a wealth of circumstance.

We must transcribe her story: "Thou didst swear to me upon a parcel-gilt goblet, sitting in my Dolphin-chamber, at the round table, by a sea-coal fire, upon Wednesday in Whitsun-Week, when the Prince broke thy head for liking his father to a singing-man of Windsor; thou didst swear to me then, as I was washing thy wound, to marry me, and make me my lady thy wife. Canst thou deny it? Did not goodwife Keech, the butcher's wife, come in then, and call me Gossip Quickly? coming in to borrow a mess of vinegar; telling us she had a good dish of prawns; whereby thou didst desire to eat some; whereby I told thee they were ill for a green wound? And didst thou not, when she was gone downstairs, desire me to be no more familiarity with such poor people; saying ere long they should call me madam? And didst thou not kiss me, and bid me fetch thee thirty shillings? I put thee now to thy book-oath; deny it if thou canst!"

We feel no doubt that if Mistress Quickly had given this evidence in action for breach of promise of marriage, and goodwife Keech corroborated it, the jury would have found a verdict for the plaintiff, unless indeed they brought in a special verdict to the effect that Falstaff made the promise, but never intended to keep it. But Mistress Quickly contented herself with upbraiding Falstaff, and he cajoled her with his usual skill, and borrowed more money of her.

Falstaff's attachment for Doll Tearsheet lasted many years, but did not lead to matrimony. From the Clement's Inn days till he was three-score he lived in London celibate, and his habits and amusements were much like those of other single gentlemen about town of his time, or, for that matter, of ours. He had only himself to care for, and he cared for himself well. Like his page, he had a good angel about him, but the devil outbid him. He was as virtuously given as other folk, but perhaps the devil had a handle for temptation in that congenital thirst of his. He was a social spirit too, and he tells us that company, villainous company, was the spoil of him. He was less than thirty when he took the faithful Bardolph into his service, and only just past that age when he made the acquaintance of the nimble Poins. Before he was forty he became the constant guest of Mistress Quickly. Pistol and Nym were later acquisitions, and the Prince did not come upon the scene till Falstaff was an old man and knighted.

There is some doubt as to when he obtained this honour. Richard II. bestowed titles in so lavish a manner as to cause discontent among many who didn't receive them. In 1377, immediately on his accession, the earldom of Nottingham was given to Thomas Mowbray, and on the same day three other earls and nine knights were created. We have not been able to discover the names of these knights, but we confidently expect to unearth them some day, and to find the name of Sir John Falstaff among them. We have already stated that Falstaff had done no service in the field at this time, so he could not have earned his title in that manner. No doubt he got it through the influence of Mowbray, who was in a position to get good things for his friends as well as for himself. It was but a poor acknowledgment for the inestimable benefit of occasionally talking with Falstaff over a quart of sack.

We will not pursue Falstaff's life further than this. It can from this point be easily collected. It is a thankless task to paraphrase a great and familiar text. To attempt to tell the story in better words than Shakespeare would occur to no one but Miss Braddon, who has epitomised Sir Walter, or to Canon Farrar, who has elongated the Gospels. But we feel bound to add a few words as to character. There are, we fear, a number of people who regard Falstaff as a worthless fellow, and who would refrain (if they could) from laughing at his jests. These people do not understand his claim

to grateful and affectionate regard. He did more
to produce that mental condition of which laughter
is the expression than any man who ever lived. But
for the cheering presence of him, and men like him,
this vale of tears would be a more terrible dwelling-
place than it is. In short, Falstaff has done an
immense deal to alleviate misery and promote
positive happiness. What more can be said of
your heroes and philanthropists?

It is, perhaps, characteristic of this commercial
age that benevolence should be always associated,
if not considered synonymous, with the giving of
money. But this is clearly mistaken, for we have
to consider what effect the money given produces
on the minds and bodies of human beings. Sir
Richard Whittington was an eminently benevolent
man, and spent his money freely for the good of
his fellow-citizens. (We sincerely hope, by the
way, that he lent some of it to Falstaff without
security.) He endowed hospitals and other
charities. Hundreds were relieved by his gifts,
and thousands (perhaps) are now in receipt of his
alms. This is well. Let the sick and the poor, who
enjoy his hospitality and receive his doles, bless
his memory. But how much wider and further-
reaching is the influence of Falstaff! Those who
enjoy his good things are not only the poor and
the sick, but all who speak the English language.
Nay, more; translation has made him the in-
heritance of the world, and the benefactor of
the entire human race.

It may be, however, that some other nations fail fully to understand and appreciate the mirth and the character of the man. A Dr. G. G. Gervinus, of Heidelberg, has written, in the German language, a heavy work on Shakespeare, in which he attacks Falstaff in a very solemn and determined manner, and particularly charges him with selfishness and want of conscience. We are inclined to set down this malignant attack to envy. Falstaff is the author and cause of universal laughter. Dr. Gervinus will never be the cause of anything universal; but, so far as his influence extends, he produces headaches. It is probably a painful sense of this contrast that goads on the author of headaches to attack the author of laughter.

But is there anything in the charge? We do not claim anything like perfection, or even saintliness, for Falstaff. But we may say of him, as Byron says of Venice, that his very vices are of the gentler sort. And as for this charge of selfishness and want of conscience, we think that the words of Bardolph on his master's death are an overwhelming answer to it. Bardolph said, on hearing the news: " I would I were with him wheresoever he is: whether he be in heaven or hell." Bardolph was a mere serving-man, not of the highest sensibility, and he for thirty years knew his master as his valet knows the hero. Surely the man who could draw such an expression of feeling from his rough servant is not the man to be lightly charged with selfishness!

Which of us can hope for such an epitaph, not from a hireling, but from our nearest and dearest? Does Dr. Gervinus know any one who will make such a reply to a posthumous charge against him of dullness and lack of humour?

RAMBLINGS IN CHEAPSIDE [1]

By Samuel Butler

WALKING the other day in Cheapside I saw some turtles in Mr. Sweeting's window, and was tempted to stay and look at them. As I did so I was struck not more by the defences with which they were hedged about, than by the fatuousness of trying to hedge that in at all which, if hedged thoroughly, must die of its own defencefulness. The holes for the head and feet through which the turtle leaks out, as it were, on to the exterior world, and through which it again absorbs the exterior world into itself—" catching on " through them to things that are thus both turtle and not turtle at one and the same time—these holes stultify the armour, and show it to have been designed by a creature with more of faithfulness to a fixed idea, and hence onesidedness, than of that quick sense of relative importances and their changes, which is the main factor of good living.

The turtle obviously had no sense of proportion; it differed so widely from myself that I could not comprehend it; and as this word occurred to me, it occurred also that until my body comprehended

[1] *Universal Review,* December 1890.

its body in a physical, material sense, neither would my mind be able to comprehend its mind with any thoroughness. For unity of mind can only be consummated by unity of body; everything, therefore, must be in some respects both knave and fool to all that which has not eaten it, or by which it has not been eaten. As long as the turtle was in the window and I in the street outside, there was no chance of our comprehending one another.

Nevertheless I knew that I could get it to agree with me if I could so effectually buttonhole and fasten on to it as to eat it. Most men have an easy method with turtle soup, and I had no misgiving but that if I could bring my first premise to bear I should prove the better reasoner. My difficulty lay in this initial process, for I had not with me the argument that would alone compel Mr. Sweeting to think that I ought to be allowed to convert the turtles—I mean I had no money in my pocket. No missionary enterprise can be carried on without any money at all, but even so small a sum as half-a-crown would, I suppose, have enabled me to bring the turtle partly round, and with many half-crowns I could in time no doubt convert the lot, for the turtle needs must go where the money drives. If, as is alleged, the world stands on a turtle, the turtle stands on money. No money no turtle. As for money, that stands on opinion, credit, trust, faith—things that, though highly material in connection with money, are still of immaterial essence.

The steps are perfectly plain. The men who caught the turtles brought a fairly strong and definite opinion to bear upon them, that passed into action, and later on into money. They thought the turtles would come that way, and verified their opinion; on this, will and action were generated, with the result that the men turned the turtles on their backs and carried them off. Mr. Sweeting touched these men with money, which is the outward and visible sign of verified opinion. The customer touches Mr. Sweeting with money, Mr. Sweeting touches the waiter and the cook with money. They touch the turtle with skill and verified opinion. Finally, the customer applies the clinching argument that brushes all sophisms aside, and bids the turtle stand protoplasm to protoplasm with himself, to know even as it is known.

But it must be all touch, touch, touch; skill, opinion, power, and money, passing in and out with one another in any order we like, but still link to link and touch to touch. If there is failure anywhere in respect of opinion, skill, power, or money, either as regards quantity or quality, the chain can be no stronger than its weakest link, and the turtle and the clinching argument will fly asunder. Of course, if there is an initial failure in connexion, through defect in any member of the chain, or of connexion between the links, it will no more be attempted to bring the turtle and the clinching argument together, than it will to chain up a dog with two pieces of broken chain that are disconnected. The contact throughout must be conceived as absolute; and yet perfect contact is inconceivable by us, for on becoming perfect it ceases to be contact, and becomes essential, once for all inseverable, identity. The most absolute contact short of this is still contact by courtesy only. So here, as everywhere else, Eurydice glides off as we are about to grasp her. We can see nothing face to face; our utmost seeing is but a fumbling of blind finger-ends in an overcrowded pocket.

Presently my own blind finger-ends fished up the conclusion, that as I had neither time nor money to spend on perfecting the chain that would put me in full spiritual contact with Mr. Sweeting's turtles, I had better leave them to complete their education at some one else's expense rather than mine, so I walked on towards the Bank. As I did so it struck me how continually we are met by this melting of one existence into another. The limits of the body seem well defined enough as definitions go, but definitions seldom go far. What, for example, can seem more distinct from a man than his banker or his solicitor? Yet these are commonly so much parts of him that he can no more cut them off and grow new ones, than he can grow new legs or arms; neither must he wound his solicitor; a wound in the solicitor is a very serious thing. As for his bank—failure of his bank's action may be as fatal to a man as failure of his heart. I have said nothing about the medical or spiritual adviser, but most men grow into the society that surrounds them by the help of these four main tap-roots, and not only into the world of humanity, but into the universe at large. We can, indeed, grow butchers, bakers, and green-grocers, almost *ad libitum*, but these are low developments, and correspond to skin, hair, or finger-nails. Those of us again who are not highly enough organised to have grown a solicitor or banker can generally repair the loss of whatever social organisation they may possess as freely as lizards are said to grow new tails; but this with the higher social, as well as organic, developments is only possible to a very limited extent.

The doctrine of metempsychosis, or transmigration of souls—a doctrine to which the foregoing considerations are for the most part easy corollaries —crops up no matter in what direction we allow our thoughts to wander. And we meet instances of transmigration of body as well as of soul. I do not mean that both body and soul have trans migrated together, far from it; but that, as we can often recognise a transmigrated mind in an alien body, so we not less often see a body that is clearly only a transmigration, linked on to some one else's new and alien soul. We meet people every day whose bodies are evidently those of men and women long dead, but whose appearance we know through their portraits. We see them going about in omnibuses, railway carriages, and in all public places. The cards have been shuffled, and they have drawn fresh lots in life and nationalities, but any one fairly well up in mediæval and last century portraiture knows them at a glance.

Going down once towards Italy I saw a young man in the train whom I recognised, only he seemed to have got younger. He was with a friend, and his face was in continual play, but for some little time I puzzled in vain to recollect where it was that I had seen him before. All of a sudden I remembered he was King Francis I. of France. I had hitherto thought the face of this king impossible, but when I saw it in play I understood it. His great contemporary Henry VIII. keeps a restaurant in Oxford Street. Falstaff drove one of the St. Gothard diligences for many years, and only retired when the railway was opened. Titian once made me a pair of boots at Vicenza, and not very good ones. At Modena I had my hair cut by a young man whom I perceived to be Raffaelle. The model who sat to him for his celebrated Madonnas is first lady in a confectionery establishment at Montreal. She has a little motherly pimple on the left side of her nose that is misleading at first, but on examination she is readily recognised; probably Raffaelle's model had the pimple too, but Raffaelle left it out—as he would.

Handel, of course, is Madame Patey. Give Madame Patey Handel's wig and clothes, and there would be no telling her from Handel. It is not only that the features and the shape of the

head are the same, but there is a certain imperiousness of expression and attitude about Handel
which he hardly attempts to conceal in Madame
Patey. It is a curious coincidence that he should
continue to be such an incomparable renderer of
his own music. Pope Julius II. was the late Mr.
Darwin. Rameses II. is a blind woman now, and
stands in Holborn, holding a tin mug. I never
could understand why I always found myself
humming " They oppressed them with burthens "
when I passed her, till one day I was looking in
Mr. Spooner's window in the Strand, and saw a
photograph of Rameses II. Mary Queen of Scots
wears surgical boots and is subject to fits, near the
Horse Shoe in Tottenham Court Road.

Michael Angelo is a commissionaire; I saw him
on board the *Glen Rosa*, which used to run every
day from London to Clacton-on-Sea and back. It
gave me quite a turn when I saw him coming down
the stairs from the upper deck, with his bronzed
face, flattened nose, and with the familiar bar upon
his forehead. I never liked Michael Angelo, and
never shall, but I am afraid of him, and was near
trying to hide when I saw him coming towards me.
He had not got his commissionaire's uniform on,
and I did not know he was one till I met him a
month or so later in the Strand. When we got to
Blackwall the music struck up and people began
to dance. I never saw a man dance so much in
my life. He did not miss a dance all the way to
Clacton, nor all the way back again, and when

not dancing he was flirting and cracking jokes. I could hardly believe my eyes when I reflected that this man had painted the famous " Last Judgment," and had made all those statues.

Dante is, or was a year or two ago, a waiter at Brissago on the Lago Maggiore, only he is better-tempered-looking, and has a more intellectual expression. He gave me his ideas upon beauty: " Tutto ch' è vero è bello," he exclaimed, with all his old self-confidence. I am not afraid of Dante. I know people by their friends, and he went about with Virgil, so I said with some severity, " No, Dante, il naso della Signora Robinson è vero, ma non è bello "; and he admitted I was right. Beatrice's name is Towler; she is waitress at a small inn in German Switzerland. I used to sit at my window and hear people call " Towler, Towler, Towler," fifty times in a forenoon. She was the exact antithesis to Abra; Abra, if I remember, used to come before they called her name, but no matter how often they called Towler, every one came before she did. I suppose they spelt her name Taula, but to me it sounded Towler; I never, however, met any one else with this name. She was a sweet, artless little hussy, who made me play the piano to her, and she said it was lovely. Of course I only played my own compositions ; so I believed her, and it all went off very nicely. I thought it might save trouble if I did not tell her who she really was, so I said nothing about it.

I met Socrates once. He was my muleteer on an excursion which I will not name, for fear it should identify the man. The moment I saw my guide I knew he was somebody, but for the life of me I could not remember who. All of a sudden it flashed across me that he was Socrates. He talked enough for six, but it was all in *dialetto*, so I could not understand him, nor, when I had discovered who he was, did I much try to do so. He was a good creature, a trifle given to stealing fruit and vegetables, but an amiable man enough. He had had a long day with his mule and me, and he only asked me five francs. I gave him ten, for I pitied his poor old patched boots, and there was a meekness about him that touched me. " And now, Socrates," said I at parting, " we go on our several ways, you to steal tomatoes, I to filch ideas from other people; for the rest—which of these two roads will be the better going, our father which is in heaven knows, but we know not."

I have never seen Mendelssohn, but there is a fresco of him on the terrace, or open-air dining-room, of an inn at Chiavenna. He is not called Mendelssohn, but I knew him by his legs. He is in the costume of a dandy of some five-and-forty years age, is smoking a cigar, and appears to be making an offer of marriage to his cook. Beethoven both my friend Mr. H. Festing Jones and I have had the good fortune to meet; he is an engineer now, and does not know one note from another; he has quite lost his deafness, is married, and is,

of course, a little squat man with the same refrac-
tory hair that he always had. It was very interesting to watch him, and Jones remarked that before
the end of dinner he had become positively posthumous. One morning I was told the Beethovens
were going away, and before long I met their two
heavy boxes being carried down the stairs. The
boxes were so squab and like their owners, that I
half thought for a moment that they were inside,
and should hardly have been surprised to see them
spring up like a couple of Jacks-in-the-box. "Sono
indentro?" said I, with a frown of wonder, pointing
to the boxes. The porters knew what I meant, and
laughed. But there is no end to the list of people
whom I have been able to recognise, and before I
had got through it myself, I found I had walked
some distance, and had involuntarily paused in
front of a second-hand bookstall.

I do not like books. I believe I have the smallest
library of any literary man in London, and I have
no wish to increase it. I keep my books at the
British Museum and at Mudie's, and it makes me
very angry if any one gives me one for my private
library. I once heard two ladies disputing in a
railway carriage as to whether one of them had
or had not been wasting money. "I spent it in
books," said the accused, "and it's not wasting
money to buy books." "Indeed, my dear, I think
it is," was the rejoinder, and in practice I agree
with it. Webster's *Dictionary*, Whitaker's *Alma-
nack*, and Bradshaw's *Railway Guide* should be

sufficient for any ordinary library; it will be time enough to go beyond these when the mass of useful and entertaining matter which they provide has been mastered. Nevertheless, I admit that sometimes, if not particularly busy, I stop at a second-hand bookstall and turn over a book or two from mere force of habit.

I know not what made me pick up a copy of Æschylus—of course in an English version—or rather I know not what made Æschylus take up with me, for he took me rather than I him; but no sooner had he got me than he began puzzling me, as he has done any time this forty years, to know wherein his transcendent merit can be supposed to lie. To me he is, like the greater number of classics in all ages and countries, a literary Struldbrug, rather than a true ambrosia-fed immortal. There are true immortals, but they are few and far between; most classics are as great impostors dead as they were when living, and while posing as gods are, five-sevenths of them, only Struldbrugs. It comforts me to remember that Aristophanes liked Æschylus no better than I do. True, he praises him by comparison with Sophocles and Euripides, but he only does so that he may run down these last more effectively. Aristophanes is a safe man to follow, nor do I see why it should not be as correct to laugh with him as to pull a long face with the Greek Professors; but this is neither here nor there, for no one really cares about Æschylus; the more interesting

question is how he contrived to make so many people for so many years pretend to care about him.

Perhaps he married somebody's daughter. If
a man would get hold of the public ear, he must
pay, marry, or fight. I have never understood that
Æschylus was a man of means, and the fighters
do not write poetry, so I suppose he must have
married a theatrical manager's daughter, and got
his plays brought out that way. The ear of any
age or country is like its land, air, and water; it
seems limitless but is really limited, and is already
in the keeping of those who naturally enough will
have no squatting on such valuable property. It
is written and talked up to as closely as the means
of subsistence are bred up to by a teeming population. There is not a square inch of it but is in
private hands, and he who would freehold any
part of it must do so by purchase, marriage, or
fighting, in the usual way—and fighting gives the
longest, safest tenure. The public itself has hardly
more voice in the question who shall have its ear,
than the land has in choosing its owners. It is
farmed as those who own it think most profitable
to themselves, and small blame to them; nevertheless, it has a residuum of mulishness which the
land has not, and does sometimes dispossess its
tenants. It is in this residuum that those who
fight place their hope and trust.

Or perhaps Æschylus squared the leading critics
of his time. When one comes to think of it, he must
have done so, for how is it conceivable that such

plays should have had such runs if he had not? I met a lady one year in Switzerland who had some parrots that always travelled with her and were the idols of her life. These parrots would not let any one read aloud in their presence, unless they heard their own names introduced from time to time. If these were freely interpolated into the text they would remain as still as stones, for they thought the reading was about themselves. If it was not about them it could not be allowed. The leaders of literature are like these parrots; they do not look at what a man writes, nor if they did would they understand it much better than the parrots do; but they like the sound of their own names, and if these are freely interpolated in a tone they take as friendly, they may even give ear to an outsider. Otherwise they will scream him off if they can.

I should not advise any one with ordinary independence of mind to attempt the public ear unless he is confident that he can out-lung and out-last his own generation; for if he has any force, people will and ought to be on their guard against him, inasmuch as there is no knowing where he may not take them. Besides, they have staked their money on the wrong men so often without suspecting it, that when there comes one whom they do suspect it would be madness not to bet against him. True, he may die before he has out-screamed his opponents, but that has nothing to do with it. If his scream was well pitched it will sound clearer when he is dead. We do not know what death is. If we know so little about life which we have experienced, how shall we know about death which we have not—and in the nature of things never can? Every one, as I said years ago in *Alps and Sanctuaries*, is an immortal to himself, for he cannot know that he is dead until he is dead, and when dead how can he know anything about anything? All we know is, that even the humblest dead may live long after all trace of the body has disappeared; we see them doing it in the bodies and memories of those that come after them; and not a few live so much longer and more effectually than is desirable, that it has been necessary to get rid of them by Act of Parliament. It is love that alone gives life, and the truest life is that which we live not in ourselves but vicariously in others, and with which we have no concern. Our concern is so to order ourselves that we may be of the number of them that enter into life—although we know it not.

Æschylus did so order himself; but his life is not of that inspiriting kind that can be won through fighting the good fight only—or being believed to have fought it. His voice is the echo of a drone, drone-begotten and drone-sustained. It is not a tone that a man must utter or die—nay, even though he die; and likely enough half the allusions and hard passages in Æschylus of which we can make neither head nor tail are in reality only puffs of some of the literary leaders of his time.

The lady above referred to told me more about her parrots. She was like a Nasmyth's hammer going slow—very gentle, but irresistible. She always read the newspaper to them. What was the use of having a newspaper if one did not read it to one's parrots?

"And have you divined," I asked, "to which side they incline in politics?"

"They do not like Mr. Gladstone," was the somewhat freezing answer; "this is the only point on which we disagree, for I adore him. Don't ask more about this, it is a great grief to me. I tell them everything," she continued, "and hide no secret from them."

"But can any parrot be trusted to keep a secret?"

"Mine can."

"And on Sundays do you give them the same course of reading as on a week-day, or do you make a difference?"

"On Sundays I always read them a genealogical chapter from the Old or New Testament, for I can thus introduce their names without profanity. I always keep tea by me in case they should ask for it in the night, and I have an Etna to warm it for them; they take milk and sugar. The old white-headed clergyman came to see them last night; it was very painful, for Jocko reminded him so strongly of his late . . ."

I thought she was going to say "wife," but it proved to have been only of a parrot that he had once known and loved.

One evening she was in difficulties about the quarantine, which was enforced that year on the Italian frontier. The local doctor had gone down that morning to see the Italian doctor and arrange some details. "Then, perhaps, my dear," she said to her husband, "he is the quarantine." "No, my love," replied her husband. "The quarantine is not a person, it is a place where they put people"; but she would not be comforted, and suspected the quarantine as an enemy that might at any moment pounce out upon her and her parrots. So a lady told me once that she had been in like trouble about the anthem. She read in her prayer-book that in choirs and places where they sing "here followeth the anthem," yet the person with this most mysteriously sounding name never did follow. They had a choir, and no one could say the church was not a place where they sang, for they did sing —both chants and hymns. Why, then, this persistent slackness on the part of the anthem, who at this juncture should follow her papa, the rector, into the reading-desk? No doubt he would come some day, and then what would he be like? Fair or dark? Tall or short? Would he be bald and wear spectacles like papa, or would he be young and good-looking? Anyhow, there was something wrong, for it was announced that he would follow, and he never did follow; therefore there was no knowing what he might not do next.

I heard of the parrots a year or two later as giving lessons in Italian to an English maid. I do not know what their terms were. Alas! since then both they and their mistress have joined the majority. When the poor lady felt her end was near she desired (and the responsibility for this must rest with her, not me) that the birds might be destroyed, as fearing that they might come to be neglected, and knowing that they could never be loved again as she had loved them. On being told that all was over, she said, "Thank you," and immediately expired.

Reflecting in such random fashion, and strolling with no greater method, I worked my way back through Cheapside and found myself once more in front of Sweeting's window. Again the turtles attracted me. They were alive, and so far at any rate they agreed with me. Nay, they had eyes, mouths, legs, if not arms, and feet, so there was much in which we were both of a mind, but surely they must be mistaken in arming themselves so very heavily. Any creature on getting what the turtle aimed at would overreach itself and be landed not in safety but annihilation. It should have no communion with the outside world at all, for death could creep in wherever the creature could creep out; and it must creep out somewhere if it was to hook on to outside things. What death can be more absolute than such absolute isolation? Perfect death, indeed, if it were attainable (which it is not), is as near perfect security as we can reach, but it is not the kind of security aimed at by any animal that is at the pains of defending itself. For such want to have things both ways, desiring the livingness of life without its perils, and the safety of death without its deadness, and some of us do actually get this for a considerable time, but we do not get it by plating ourselves with armour as the turtle does. We tried this in the Middle Ages, and no longer mock ourselves with the weight of armour that our forefathers carried in battle. Indeed the more deadly the weapons of attack become the more we go into the fight slug-wise.

Slugs have ridden their contempt for defensive armour as much to death as the turtles their pursuit of it. They have hardly more than skin enough to hold themselves together; they court death every time they cross the road. Yet death comes not to them more than to the turtle, whose defences are so great that there is little left inside to be defended. Moreover, the slugs fare best in the long run, for turtles are dying out, while slugs are not, and there must be millions of slugs all the world over for every single turtle. Of the two vanities, therefore, that of the slug seems most substantial.

In either case the creature thinks itself safe, but is sure to be found out sooner or later; nor is it easy to explain this mockery save by reflecting that everything must have its meat in due season, and that meat can only be found for such a multitude of mouths by giving everything as meat in due season to something else. This is like the Kilkenny cats, or robbing Peter to pay Paul; but it is the way of the world, and as every animal must contribute in kind to the picnic of the universe, one does not see what better arrangement could be made than the providing each race with a hereditary fallacy, which shall in the end get it into a scrape, but which shall generally stand the wear and tear of life for some time. " Do ut des " is the writing on all flesh to him that eats it; and no creature is dearer to itself than it is to some other that would devour it.

Nor is there any statement or proposition more invulnerable than living forms are. Propositions prey upon and are grounded upon one another just like living forms. They support one another as plants and animals do; they are based ultimately on credit, or faith, rather than the cash of irrefragable conviction. The whole universe is carried on on the credit system, and if the mutual confidence on which it is based were to collapse, it must itself collapse immediately. Just or unjust, it lives by faith; it is based on vague and impalpable opinion that by some inscrutable process passes into will and action, and is made manifest in matter and in flesh: it is meteoric—suspended in mid-air; it is the baseless fabric of a vision so vast, so vivid, and so gorgeous that no base can seem more broad than such stupendous baselessness, and yet any man can bring it about his ears by being over-curious; when faith fails a system based on faith fails also.

Whether the universe is really a paying concern,

or whether it is an inflated bubble that must burst sooner or later, this is another matter. If people were to demand cash payment in irrefragable certainty for everything that they have taken hitherto as paper money on the credit of the bank of public opinion, is there money enough behind it all to stand so great a drain even on so great a reserve? Probably there is not, but happily there can be no such panic, for even though the cultured classes may do so, the uncultured are too dull to have brains enough to commit such stupendous folly. It takes a long course of academic training to educate a man up to the standard which he must reach before he can entertain such questions seriously, and by a merciful dispensation of Providence, university training is almost as costly as it is unprofitable. The majority will thus be always unable to afford it, and will base their opinions on mother-wit and current opinion rather than on demonstration.

So I turned my steps homewards; I saw a good many more things on my way home, but I was told that I was not to see more this time than I could get into twelve pages of the *Universal Review*; l must therefore reserve any remark which I think might perhaps entertain the reader for another occasion.

WALKING TOURS

By Robert Louis Stevenson

IT must not be imagined that a walking tour, as some would have us fancy, is merely a better or worse way of seeing the country. There are many ways of seeing landscape quite as good; and none more vivid, in spite of canting dilettantes, than from a railway train. But landscape on a walking tour is quite accessory. He who is indeed of the brotherhood does not voyage in quest of the picturesque, but of certain jolly humours—of the hope and spirit with which the march begins at morning, and the peace and spiritual repletion of the evening's rest. He cannot tell whether he puts his knapsack on, or takes it off, with more delight. The excitement of the departure puts him in key for that of the arrival. Whatever he does is not only a reward in itself, but will be further rewarded in the sequel; and so pleasure leads on to pleasure in an endless chain. It is this that so few can understand; they will either be always lounging or always at five miles an hour; they do not play off the one against the other, prepare all day for the evening, and all evening for the next day. And, above all, it is here that your overwalker fails of comprehension. His heart rises against those who drink their curaçoa in liqueur glasses, when he himself can swill it in a brown john. He will not believe that the flavour is more delicate in the smaller dose. He will not believe that to walk this unconscionable distance is merely to stupefy and brutalise himself, and come to his inn, at night, with a sort of frost on his five wits, and a starless night of darkness in his spirit. Not for him the mild luminous evening of the temperate walker! He has nothing left of man but a physical need for bedtime and a double nightcap; and even his pipe, if he be a smoker, will be savourless and disenchanted. It is the fate of such an one to take twice as much trouble as is needed to obtain happiness, and miss the happiness in the end; he is the man of the proverb, in short, who goes further and fares worse.

Now, to be properly enjoyed, a walking tour should be gone upon alone. If you go in a company, or even in pairs, it is no longer a walking tour in anything but name; it is something else and more in the nature of a picnic. A walking tour should be gone upon alone, because freedom is of the essence; because you should be able to stop and go on, and follow this way or that, as the freak takes you; and because you must have your own pace, and neither trot alongside a champion walker, nor mince in time with a girl. And then you must be open to all impressions and let your thoughts take colour from what you see. You should be as

a pipe for any wind to play upon. " I cannot see
the wit," says Hazlitt, " of walking and talking
at the same time. When I am in the country I
wish to vegetate like the country,"—which is the
gist of all that can be said upon the matter. There
should be no cackle of voices at your elbow, to jar
on the meditative silence of the morning. And so
long as a man is reasoning he cannot surrender
himself to that fine intoxication that comes of
much motion in the open air, that begins in a sort
of dazzle and sluggishness of the brain, and ends
in a peace that passes comprehension.

During the first day or so of any tour there are
moments of bitterness, when the traveller feels
more than coldly towards his knapsack, when he
is half in a mind to throw it bodily over the hedge
and, like Christian on a similar occasion, " give
three leaps and go on singing." And yet it soon
acquires a property of easiness. It becomes mag-
netic; the spirit of the journey enters into it. And
no sooner have you passed the straps over your
shoulder than the lees of sleep are cleared from
you, you pull yourself together with a shake, and
fall at once into your stride. And surely, of all
possible moods, this, in which a man takes the
road, is the best. Of course, if he *will* keep thinking
of his anxieties, if he *will* open the merchant
Abudah's chest and walk arm-in-arm with the
hag—why, wherever he is, and whether he walk
fast or slow, the chances are that he will not be
happy. And so much the more shame to himself!

There are perhaps thirty men setting forth at that same hour, and I would lay a large wager there is not another dull face among the thirty. It would be a fine thing to follow, in a coat of darkness, one after another of these wayfarers, some summer morning, for the first few miles upon the road. This one, who walks fast, with a keen look in his eyes, is all concentrated in his own mind; he is up at his loom, weaving and weaving, to set the landscape to words. This one peers about, as he goes, among the grasses; he waits by the canal to watch the dragon-flies; he leans on the gate of the pasture, and cannot look enough upon the complacent kine. And here comes another, talking, laughing, and gesticulating to himself. His face changes from time to time, as indignation flashes from his eyes or anger clouds his forehead. He is composing articles, delivering orations, and conducting the most impassioned interviews, by the way. A little farther on, and it is as like as not he will begin to sing. And well for him, supposing him to be no great master in that art, if he stumble across no stolid peasant at a corner; for on such an occasion, I scarcely know which is the more troubled, or whether it is worse to suffer the confusion of your troubadour, or the unfeigned alarm of your clown. A sedentary population, accustomed, besides, to the strange mechanical bearing of the common tramp, can in no wise explain to itself the gaiety of these passers-by. I knew one man who was arrested as a runaway lunatic, because, although a full-grown person with a red beard, he skipped as he went like a child. And you would be astonished if I were to tell you all the grave and learned heads who have confessed to me that, when on walking tours, they sang—and sang very ill—and had a pair of red ears when, as described above, the inauspicious peasant plumped into their arms from round a corner. And here, lest you should think I am exaggerating, is Hazlitt's own confession, from his essay *On Going a Journey*, which is so good that there should be a tax levied on all who have not read it:

" Give me the clear blue sky over my head," says he, " and the green turf beneath my feet, a winding road before me, and a three hours' march to dinner—and then to thinking! It is hard if I cannot start some game on these lone heaths. I laugh, I run, I leap, I sing for joy."

Bravo! After that adventure of my friend with the policeman, you would not have cared, would you, to publish that in the first person? But we have no bravery nowadays, and, even in books, must all pretend to be as dull and foolish as our neighbours. It was not so with Hazlitt. And notice how learned he is (as, indeed, throughout the essay) in the theory of walking tours. He is none of your athletic men in purple stockings, who walk their fifty miles a day: three hours' march is his ideal. And then he must have a winding road, the epicure!

Yet there is one thing I object to in these words

of his, one thing in the great master's practice that seems to me not wholly wise. I do not approve of that leaping and running. Both of these hurry the respiration; they both shake up the brain out of its glorious 'open-air confusion; and they both break the pace. Uneven walking is not so agreeable to the body, and it distracts and irritates the mind. Whereas, when once you have fallen into an equable stride, it requires no conscious thought from you to keep it up, and yet it prevents you from thinking earnestly of anything else. Like knitting, like the work of a copying clerk, it gradually neutralises and sets to sleep the serious activity of the mind. We can think of this or that, lightly and laughingly, as a child thinks, or as we think in a morning doze; we can make puns or puzzle out acrostics, and trifle in a thousand ways with words and rhymes; but when it comes to honest work, when we come to gather ourselves together for an effort, we may sound the trumpet as loud and long as we please; the great barons of the mind will not rally to the standard, but sit, each one, at home, warming his hands over his own fire and brooding on his own private thought!

In the course of a day's walk, you see, there is much variance in the mood. From the exhilaration of the start, to the happy phlegm of the arrival, the change is certainly great. As the day goes on, the traveller moves from the one extreme towards the other. He becomes more and more incorporated with the material landscape, and the open-air drunkenness grows upon him with great strides, until he posts along the road, and sees everything about him, as in a cheerful dream. The first is certainly brighter, but the second stage is the more peaceful. A man does not make so many articles towards the end, nor does he laugh aloud; but the purely animal pleasures, the sense of physical wellbeing, the delight of every inhalation, of every time the muscles tighten down the thigh, console him for the absence of the others, and bring him to his destination still content.

Nor must I forget to say a word on bivouacs. You come to a milestone on a hill, or some place where deep ways meet under trees; and off goes the knapsack, and down you sit to smoke a pipe in the shade. You sink into yourself, and the birds come round and look at you; and your smoke dissipates upon the afternoon under the blue dome of heaven; and the sun lies warm upon your feet, and the cool air visits your neck and turns aside your open shirt. If you are not happy, you must have an evil conscience. You may dally as long as you like by the roadside. It is almost as if the millennium were arrived, when we shall throw our clocks and watches over the housetop, and remember time and seasons no more. Not to keep hours for a lifetime is, I was going to say, to live for ever. You have no idea, unless you have tried it, how endlessly long is a summer's day, that you measure out only by hunger, and bring to an end only when you are drowsy. I know a village where there are hardly any clocks, where no one knows more of the days of the week than by a sort of instinct for the fête on Sundays, and where only one person can tell you the day of the month, and she is generally wrong; and if people were aware how slow Time journeyed in that village, and what armfuls of spare hours he gives, over and above the bargain, to its wise inhabitants, I believe there would be a stampede out of London, Liverpool, Paris, and a variety of large towns, where the clocks lose their heads, and shake the hours out each one faster than the other, as though they were all in a wager. And all these foolish pilgrims would each bring his own misery along with him, in a watch-pocket! It is to be noticed, there were no clocks and watches in the much-vaunted days before the flood. It follows, of course, there were no appointments, and punctuality was not yet thought upon. "Though ye take from a covetous man all his treasure," says Milton, " he has yet one jewel left; ye cannot deprive him of his covetousness." And so I would say of a modern man of business, you may do what you will for him, put him in Eden, give him the elixir of life—he has still a flaw at heart, he still has his business habits. Now, there is no time when business habits are more mitigated than on a walking tour. And so during these halts, as I say, you will feel almost free.

But it is at night, and after dinner, that the best hour comes. There are no such pipes to be smoked as those that follow a good day's march; the flavour of the tobacco is a thing to be remembered, it is so dry and aromatic, so full and so fine. If you wind up the evening with grog, you will own there was never such grog; at every sip a jocund tranquillity spreads about your limbs, and sits easily in your heart. If you read a book—and you will never do so save by fits and starts—you find the language strangely racy and harmonious; words take a new meaning; single sentences possess the ear for half an hour together; and the writer endears himself to you, at every page, by the nicest coincidence of sentiment. It seems as if it were a book you had written yourself in a dream. To all we have read on such occasions we look back with special favour. " It was on the 10th of April, 1798," says Hazlitt, with amorous precision, " that I sat down to a volume of the *New Héloïse*, at the Inn at Llangollen, over a bottle of sherry and a cold chicken." I should wish to quote more, for though we are mighty fine fellows nowadays, we cannot write like Hazlitt. And, talking of that, a volume of Hazlitt's essays would be a capital pocket-book on such a journey; so would a volume of Heine's songs; and for *Tristram Shandy* I can pledge a fair experience.

If the evening be fine and warm, there is nothing better in life than to lounge before the inn door in the sunset, or lean over the parapet of the bridge, to watch the weeds and the quick fishes. It is then, if ever, that you taste Joviality to the full signifi-

cance of that audacious word. Your muscles are
so agreeably slack, you feel so clean and so strong
and so idle, that whether you move or sit still,
whatever you do is done with pride and a kingly
sort of pleasure. You fall in talk with any one,
wise or foolish, drunk or sober. And it seems as if
a hot walk purged you, more than of anything
else, of all narrowness and pride, and left curiosity
to play its part freely, as in a child or a man of
science. You lay aside all your own hobbies, to
watch provincial humours develop themselves
before you, now as a laughable farce, and now
grave and beautiful like an old tale.

Or perhaps you are left to your own company
for the night, and surly weather imprisons you
by the fire. You may remember how Burns,
numbering past pleasures, dwells upon the hours
when he has been " happy thinking." It is a
phrase that may well perplex a poor modern, girt
about on every side by clocks and chimes, and
haunted, even at night, by flaming dial-plates.
For we are all so busy, and have so many far-off
projects to realise, and castles in the fire to turn
into solid habitable mansions on a gravel soil,
that we can find no time for pleasure trips into
the Land of Thought and among the Hills of
Vanity. Changed times, indeed, when we must
sit all night, beside the fire, with folded hands;
and a changed world for most of us, when we find
we can pass the hours without discontent, and be
happy thinking. We are in such haste to be doing,

to be writing, to be gathering gear, to make our voice audible a moment in the derisive silence of eternity, that we forget that one thing, of which these are but the parts—namely, to live. We fall in love, we drink hard, we run to and fro upon the earth like frightened sheep. And now you are to ask yourself if, when all is done, you would not have been better to sit by the fire at home, and be happy thinking. To sit still and contemplate,— to remember the faces of women without desire, to be pleased by the great deeds of men without envy, to be everything and everywhere in sympathy, and yet content to remain where and what you are—is not this to know both wisdom and virtue, and to dwell with happiness? After all, it is not they who carry flags, but they who look upon it from a private chamber, who have the fun of the procession. And once you are at that, you are in the very humour of all social heresy. It is no time for shuffling, or for big, empty words. If you ask yourself what you mean by fame, riches, or learning, the answer is far to seek; and you go back into that kingdom of light imaginations, which seem so vain in the eyes of Philistines perspiring after wealth, and so momentous to those who are stricken with the disproportions of the world, and, in the face of the gigantic stars, cannot stop to split differences between two degrees of the infinitesimally small, such as a tobacco pipe or the Roman Empire, a million of money or a fiddle-stick's end.

ROBERT LOUIS STEVENSON

You lean from the window, your last pipe reeking whitely into the darkness, your body full of delicious pains, your mind enthroned in the seventh circle of content; when suddenly the mood changes, the weathercock goes about, and you ask yourself one question more: whether, for the interval, you have been the wisest philosopher or the most egregious of donkeys? Human experience is not yet able to reply; but at least you have had a fine moment, and looked down upon all the kingdoms of the earth. And whether it was wise or foolish, to-morrow's travel will carry you, body and mind, into some different parish of the infinite.

GOLDSMITH

By Austin Dobson

THIRTY years of taking in; fifteen years of giving
out;—that, in brief, is Oliver Goldsmith's story.
When, in 1758, his failure to pass at Surgeons'
Hall finally threw him on letters for a living, the
thirty years were finished, and the fifteen years
had been begun. What was to come he knew not;
but, from his bare-walled lodging in Green-Arbour
Court, he could at least look back upon a sufficiently diversified past. He had been an idle,
orchard-robbing schoolboy; a tuneful but in-
tractable sizar of Trinity; a lounging, loitering,
fair-haunting, flute-playing Irish "buckeen." He
had tried both Law and Divinity, and crossed the
threshold of neither. He had started for London
and stopped at Dublin; he had set out for America
and arrived at Cork. He had been many things:—
a medical student, a strolling musician, a corrector
of the press, an apothecary, an usher at a Peckham
"academy." Judged by ordinary standards, he
had wantonly wasted his time. And yet, as things
fell out, it is doubtful whether his parti-coloured
experiences were not of more service to him than
any he could have obtained if his progress had
been less erratic. Had he fulfilled the modest

expectations of his family, he would probably have remained a simple curate in Westmeath, eking out his " forty pounds a year " by farming a field or two, migrating contentedly at the fitting season from the " blue bed to the brown," and (it may be) subsisting vaguely as a local poet upon the tradition of some youthful couplets to a pretty cousin, who had married a richer man. As it was, if he could not be said " to have seen life steadily, and seen it whole," he had, at all events, inspected it pretty narrowly in parts; and, at a time when he was most impressible, had preserved the impress of many things which, in his turn, he was to re-impress upon his writings. " No man "—says one of his biographers—" ever put so much of himself into his books as Goldsmith." To his last hour he was drawing upon the thoughts and reviving the memories of that " unhallowed time " when, to all appearance, he was hopelessly squandering his opportunities. To do as Goldsmith did, would scarcely enable a man to write a *Vicar of Wakefield* or a *Deserted Village*,—certainly his practice cannot be preached with safety " to those that eddy round and round." But viewing his entire career, it is difficult not to see how one part seems to have been an indispensable preparation for the other, and to marvel once more (with the philosopher Square) at " the eternal Fitness of Things."

The events of Goldsmith's life have been too often narrated to need repetition here, and we shall not

resort to the well-worn device of repeating them
in order to say so. But, in a fresh reprint of his
Poems and Plays, some brief preamble to those
branches of his work may be excusable, and even
useful. And, with regard to both, what strikes
one first is the extreme tardiness of that late blos-
soming to which Johnson referred. When a man
succeeds as Goldsmith succeeded, friends and
critics speedily discover that he had shown signs
of excellence even from his boyish years. But,
setting aside those half-mythical ballads for the
Dublin street-singers, and some doubtful verses
for Jane Contarine, there is no definite evidence
that, from a doggerel couplet in his childhood to
an epigram not much better than doggerel composed when he was five and twenty, he had written
a line of verse of the slightest importance; and
even five years later, although he refers to himself
in a private letter as a " poet," it must have been
solely upon the strength of the unpublished fragment of *The Traveller*, which in the interval, he
had sent to his brother Henry from abroad. It
is even more remarkable that—although so skilful
a correspondent must have been fully sensible of
his gifts—until, under the pressure of circumstances, he drifted into literature, the craft of
letters seems never to have been his ambition. He
thinks of being a lawyer, a physician, a clergyman,
—anything but an author; and when at last he
engages in that profession, it is to free himself
from a scholastic servitude which he appears to

have always regarded with peculiar bitterness, yet
to which, after a first unsatisfactory trial of what
was to be his true vocation, he unhesitatingly returned. If he went back once more to his pen, it
was only to enable him to escape from it more
effectually, and he was prepared to go as far as
Coromandel. But Literature—" toute entière à sa
proie attachée "—refused to relinquish him; and,
although he continued to make spasmodic efforts
to extricate himself, detained him to the day of
his death.

If there is no evidence that he had written much
when he entered upon what has been called his
second period, he had not the less formed his
opinions on many literary questions. Much of the
matter of the *Polite Learning* is plainly manufactured *ad hoc*; but in its references to authorship and
criticism, there is a personal note which is absent
elsewhere; and when he speaks of the tyranny of
publishers, the sordid standards of criticism, and
the forlorn and precarious existence of the hapless
writer for bread, he is evidently reproducing a
condition of things with which he had become
familiar during his brief bondage on the *Monthly
Review*. As to his personal views on poetry in
particular, it is easy to collect them from this, and
later utterances. Against blank verse he protests
from the first, as suited only to the sublimest
themes—which is a polite way of shelving it
altogether; while in favour of rhyme he alleges
that the very restriction stimulates the fancy, as

a fountain plays higher when the aperture is diminished. Blank verse, too (he asserted), imported into poetry a " disgusting solemnity of manner " which was fatal to " agreeable trifling," —an objection intimately connected with the feeling which afterwards made him the champion on the stage of character and humour. Among the poets who were his contemporaries and immediate predecessors, his likes and dislikes were strong. He fretted at the fashion which Gray's *Elegy* set in poetry; he considered it a fine poem, but " overloaded with epithet," and he deplored the remoteness and want of emotion which distinguished the Pindaric Odes. Yet from many indications in his own writings, he seems to have genuinely appreciated the work of Collins. Churchill, and Churchill's satire, he detested. With Young he had some personal acquaintance, and had attentively read his *Night Thoughts*. Of the poets of the last age, he admired Dryden, Pope and Gay, but more than any of these, if imitation is to be regarded as the proof of sympathy, Prior, Addison and Swift. By his inclinations and his training, indeed, he belonged to this school. But he was in advance of it in thinking that poetry, however didactic after the fashion of his own day, should be simple in its utterance and directed at the many rather than the few. This is what he meant when, from the critical elevation of Griffiths' back parlour, he recommended Gray to take the advice of Isocrates, and " study the people." If, with these

ideas, he had been able to divest himself of the
" warbling groves " and " finny deeps " of the
Popesque vocabulary (of much of the more
" mechanic art " of that supreme artificer he *did*
successfully divest himself), it would have needed
but little to make him a prominent pioneer of the
new school which was coming with Cowper. As
it is, his poetical attitude is a little that intermediate one of Longfellow's maiden—

> Standing, with reluctant feet,
> Where the brook and river meet.

Most of his minor and earlier pieces are imitative.
In *A New Simile*, and *The Logicians Refuted*
Swift is his acknowledged model; in *The Double
Transformation* it is Prior, modified by certain
theories personal to himself. He was evidently
well acquainted with collections like the *Ména-
giana*, and with the French minor poets of the
eighteenth century, many of which latter were
among his books at his death. These he had
carefully studied, probably during his continental
wanderings, and from them he derives, like Prior,
much of his grace and metrical buoyancy. The
Elegy on the Death of a Mad Dog, and *Madam
Blaize*, are both more or less constructed on the
old French popular song of the hero of Pavia,
Jacques de Chabannes, Seigneur de la Palice
(sometimes Galisse), with, in the case of the
former, a tag from an epigram by Voltaire, the
original of which is in the Greek Anthology,
though Voltaire simply " conveyed " his version

from an anonymous French predecessor. Similarly the lively stanzas *To Iris, in Bow Street*, the lines to Myra, the quatrain called *A South American Ode*, and that *On a Beautiful Youth struck blind with Lightning*, are all confessed or unconfessed translations. It is possible that if Goldsmith had lived to collect his own works, he would have announced the source of his inspiration in these instances as well as in one or two other cases—the epitaph on Ned Purdon, for example,—where it has been reserved to his editors to discover his obligations. On the other hand, he might have contended, with perfect justice, that whatever the source of his ideas, he had made them his own when he got them; and certainly in lilt and lightness, the lines *To Iris* are infinitely superior to those of La Monnoye, on which they are based. But even a fervent admirer may admit that, dwelling as he did in this very vitreous palace of Gallic adaptation, one does not expect to find him throwing stones at Prior for borrowing from the French, or commenting solemnly in the life of Parnell upon the heinousness of plagiarism. "It was the fashion," he says, "with the wits of the last age, to conceal the places from whence they took their hints or their subjects. A trifling acknowledgment would have made that lawful prize, which may now be considered as plunder." He might judiciously have added to this latter sentence the quotation which he struck out of the second issue of the *Polite Learning*,—"Haud inexpertus loquor."

Of his longer pieces, *The Traveller* was apparently suggested to him by Addison's *Letter from Italy to Lord Halifax*, a poem to which, in his preliminary notes to the *Beauties of English Poesy*, he gives significant praise. "There is in it," he says, "a strain of political thinking that was, at that time, new in our poetry." He obviously intended that *The Traveller* should be admired for the same reason; and both in that poem and its successor, *The Deserted Village*, he lays stress upon the political import of his work. The one, we are told, is to illustrate the position that the happiness of the subject is independent of the goodness of the Sovereign; the other, to deplore the increase of luxury and the miseries of depopulation. But, as a crowd of commentators have pointed out, it is hazardous for a poet to meddle with "political thinking," however much, under George the Second, it may have been needful to proclaim a serious purpose. If Goldsmith had depended solely upon the professedly didactic part of his attempt, his work would be as dead as *Freedom*, or *Sympathy*, or any other of Dodsley's forgotten *quartos*. Fortunately he did more than this. Sensibly or insensibly, he suffused his work with that philanthropy which is "not learned by the royal road of tracts, and platform speeches, and monthly magazines," but by personal commerce with poverty and sorrow; and he made his appeal to that clinging love of country, of old association of "home-bred happiness," of innocent pleasure, which, with Englishmen, is never made in vain. Employing the couplet of Pope and Johnson, he has added to his measure a suavity that belonged to neither; but the beauty of his humanity and the tender melancholy of his wistful retrospect hold us more strongly and securely than the studious finish of his style.

"Vingt fois sur le métier remettez votre ouvrage" —said the arch-critic whose name, according to Keats, the school of Pope displayed upon their "decrepit standard." Even in *The Traveller* and *The Deserted Village*, there are indications of over-labour; but in a poem which comes between them—the once famous *Edwin and Angelina*— Goldsmith certainly carried out Boileau's maxim to the full. The first privately-printed version differs considerably from that in the first edition of the *Vicar*; this again is altered in the fourth; and there are other variations in the piece as printed in the *Poems for Young Ladies*. "As to my *Hermit*," said the poet complacently, "that poem, Cradock, cannot be amended," and undoubtedly it has been skilfully wrought. But it is impossible to look upon it now with the unpurged eyes of those upon whom the *Reliques of Ancient Poetry* had but recently dawned, still less to endorse the verdict of Sir John Hawkins that "it is one of the finest poems of the lyric kind that our language has to boast of." Its over-soft prettiness is too much that of the chromo-lithograph or the Parian bust (the porcelain, not the marble), and

its " beautiful simplicity " is in parts perilously
close upon that inanity which Johnson, whose
sturdy good sense not even friendship could silence,
declared to be the characteristic of much of Percy's
collection. It is instructive as a study of poetical
progress to contrast it with a ballad of our own
day in the same measure—the *Talking Oak* of
Tennyson.

The remaining poems of Goldsmith, excluding
the *Captivity*, and the admittedly occasional
Threnodia Augustalis, are not open to the charge
of fictitious simplicity, or of that hyper-elabora-
tion, which, in the words of the poet just mentioned, makes for the " ripe and rotten." The
gallery of kit-cats in *Retaliation*, and the delightful
bonhomie of *The Haunch of Venison* need no commendation. In kindly humour and not unkindly
satire Goldsmith was at his best, and the imperish-
able portraits of Burke and Garrick and Reynolds,
and the inimitable dinner at which Lord Clare's
pasty was *not*, are as well known as any of the stock
passages of *The Deserted Village* or *The Traveller*,
though they have never been babbled " in extremis
vicis " by successive generations of schoolboys. It
is usually said, probably with truth, that in these
poems and the delightful *Letter to Mrs. Bunbury*,
Goldsmith's metre was suggested by the cantering
anapæsts of the *New Bath Guide*, and it is to be
observed that " Little Comedy's " letter of invitation is to the same popular tune. But in annotating
this edition, some inquiries as to the song of *Ally*

Croker mentioned in *She Stoops to Conquer*, elicited the fact that a line of that once popular lyric—

> Too dull for a wit, and too grave for a joker—

has a kind of echo in the—

> Too nice for a statesman, too proud for a wit—

of Burke's portrait in *Retaliation*. What is still more remarkable is that Gray's *Sketch of his own Character*, the resemblance of which to Goldsmith has been pointed out by his editors, begins—

> Too poor for a bribe, and too proud to importune.

Whether Goldsmith was thinking of Anstey or *Ally Croker*, it is at least worthy of passing notice that an Irish song of no particular literary merit should have succeeded in haunting the two foremost poets of their day.

Poetry brought Goldsmith fame, but money only indirectly. Those Saturnian days of the subscription-edition, when Pope and Gay and Prior counted their gains by thousands, were over and gone. He had arrived, it has been well said, too late for the Patron, and too early for the Public. Of his lighter pieces the best were posthumous; the rest were either paid for at hack prices or not at all. For *The Deserted Village* Griffin gave him a hundred guineas, a sum so unexampled as to have prompted the pleasant legend that he returned it. For *The Traveller* the only payment that can be definitely traced is £21. "I cannot afford to court the draggle-tail Muses," he said laughingly to Lord

Lisburn, "they would let me starve; but by my other labours I can make shift to eat, and drink, and have good clothes." It was in his "other labours" that his poems helped him. The book-sellers who would not or could not remunerate him adequately for delayed production and minute revision, were willing enough to secure the sanction of his name for humbler journey-work. If he was ill-paid for *The Traveller*, he was not ill-paid for the *Beauties of English Poesy* or the *History of Animated Nature*.

Yet, notwithstanding his ready pen, and his skill as a compiler, his life was a *métier de forçat*. "While you are nibbling about elegant phrases, I am obliged to write half a volume,"—he told his friend Cradock; and it was but natural that he should desire to escape into walks where he might accomplish something "for his own hand," by which, at the same time, he might exist. Fiction he had already essayed. Nearly two years before *The Traveller* appeared, he had written a story about the length of *Joseph Andrews*, for which he had received little more than a third of the sum paid by Andrew Millar to Fielding for his burlesque of Richardson's *Pamela*. But obscure circum-stances delayed the publication of the *Vicar of Wakefield* for four years, and when at last it was issued, its first burst of success—a success, as far as can be ascertained, productive of no further profit to its author—was followed by a long period during which the sales were languid and uncertain.

There remained the stage, with its two-fold allurement of fame and fortune, both payable at sight, added to which it was always possible that a popular play, in those days when plays were bought to read, might find a brisk market in book form. The prospect was a tempting one, and it is scarcely surprising that Goldsmith, weary of the " dry drudgery at the desk's dead wood," and conscious of better things within him, should engage in that most tantalising of all enterprises, the pursuit of dramatic success.

For acting and actors he had always shown a decided partiality.[1] Vague stories, based, in all probability, upon the references to strolling players in his writings, hinted that he himself had once worn the comic sock as " Scrub " in *The Beaux' Stratagem*; and it is clear that soon after he arrived in England, he had completed a tragedy, for he read it in manuscript to a friend. That he had been besides an acute and observant playgoer, is plain from his excellent account in *The Bee* of Mademoiselle Clairon, whom he had seen at Paris, and from his sensible notes in the same periodical on " gestic lore " as exhibited on the English stage.

---

[1] This is not inconsistent with the splenetic utterances in the letters to Daniel Hodson, first made public in the "Great Writers" *Life of Goldsmith*, where he speaks of the stage as "an abominable resource which neither became a man of honour, not a man of sense." Those letters were written when the production of *The Good-Natur'd Man* had supplied him with abundant practical evidence of the vexations and difficulties of theatrical ambition.

In his *Polite Learning in Europe*, he had followed up Ralph's *Case of Authors by Profession*, by protesting against the despotism of managers, and the unenlightened but economical policy of producing only the works of deceased playwrights; and he was equally opposed to the growing tendency on the part of the public—a tendency dating from Richardson and the French *comédie larmoyante*—to substitute sham sensibility and superficial refinement for that humorous delineation of manners, which, with all their errors of morality and taste, had been the chief aim of Congreve and his contemporaries. To the fact that what was now known as "genteel comedy" had almost wholly supplanted this elder and better manner, must be attributed his deferred entry upon a field so obviously adapted to his gifts. But when, in 1766, the *Clandestine Marriage* of Garrick and Colman, with its evergreen "Lord Ogleby," seemed to herald a return to the side of laughter as opposed to that of tears, he took heart of grace, and, calling to mind something of the old inconsiderate benevolence which had been the Goldsmith family-failing, set about his first comedy, *The Good-Natur'd Man*.

Even without experiment, no one could have known better than Goldsmith, upon what a sea of troubles he had embarked. Those obstacles which, more than thirty years before, had been so graphically described in Fielding's *Pasquin*,—which Goldsmith himself had indicated with equal accuracy in his earliest book, still lay in the way of all dramatic purpose, and he was to avoid none of them. When he submitted his completed work to Garrick, the all-powerful actor, who liked neither piece nor author, blew hot and cold so long, that Goldsmith at last, in despair, transferred it to Colman. But, as if fate was inexorable, Colman, after accepting it effusively, also grew dilatory, and ultimately entered into a tacit league with Garrick not to produce it at Covent Garden until his former rival had brought out at Drury Lane a comedy by Goldsmith's countryman, Hugh Kelly, a sentimentalist of the first water. Upon the heels of the enthusiastic reception which Garrick's administrative tact secured for the superfine *imbroglios* of *False Delicacy*, came limping *The Good-Natur'd Man* of Goldsmith, wet-blanketed beforehand by a sententious prologue from Johnson. No *début* could have been less favourable. Until it was finally saved in the fourth act by the excellent art of Shuter, its fate hung trembling in the balance, and even then one of its scenes—not afterwards reckoned the worst—had to be withdrawn in deference to the delicate scruples of an audience which could not suffer such inferior beings as bailiffs to come between the wind and its gentility. Yet, in spite of all these disadvantages, *The Good-Natur'd Man* obtained a hearing, besides bringing its author about five hundred pounds, a sum far larger than anything he had ever made by poetry or fiction.

That the superior success of *False Delicacy*, with

its mincing morality and jumble of inadequate motive, was wholly temporary and accidental, is evident from the fact that, to use a felicitous phrase, it has now to be disinterred in order to be discussed. But, notwithstanding one's instinctive sympathy for Goldsmith in his struggles with the managers, it is not equally clear that, everything considered, *The Good-Natur'd Man* was unfairly treated by the public. Because Kelly's play was praised too much, it by no means follows that Goldsmith's play was praised too little. With all the advantage of its author's reputation, it has never since passed into the *répertoire*, and, if it had something of the freshness of a first effort, it had also its inexperience. The chief character, Honeywood—the weak and amiable " good-natur'd man "—never stands very firmly on his feet, and the first actor, Garrick's promising young rival, Powell, failed, or disdained to make it a stage creation. On the other hand, " Croaker," an admitted elaboration of Johnson's sketch of " Suspirius " in the *Rambler*, is a first-rate comic character, and the charlatan " Lofty," a sort of " Beau-Tibbs-above-Stairs," is almost as good. But, as Garrick's keen eye saw, to have a second male figure of greater importance than the central personage was a serious error of judgment, added to which neither " Miss Richland " nor " Mrs. Croaker " ever establish any hold upon the audience. Last of all, the plot, such as it is, cannot be described as either particularly ingenious or particularly novel. In another way, the merit of the piece is, however, incontestable. It is written with all the perspicuous grace of Goldsmith's easy pen, and, in the absence of stage-craft, sparkles with neat and effective epigrams. One of these may be mentioned as illustrating the writer's curious (perhaps unconscious) habit of repeating ideas which had pleased him. He had quoted in his *Polite Learning* the exquisitely rhythmical close of Sir William Temple's prose essay on " Poetry," and in *The Bee* it still seems to haunt him. In *The Good-Natur'd Man* he has absorbed it altogether, for he places it, without inverted commas, in the lips of Croaker.

But, if its lack of constructive power and its errors of conception make it impossible to regard *The Good-Natur'd Man* as a substantial gain to humorous drama, it was undoubtedly a formidable attack upon that " mawkish drab of spurious breed," Sentimental Comedy, and its success was amply sufficient to justify a second trial. That Goldsmith did not forthwith make this renewed effort must be attributed partly to the recollection of his difficulties in getting his first play produced, partly to the fact that, his dramatic gains exhausted, he was almost immediately involved in a sequence of laborious taskwork. Still, he had never abandoned his ambition to restore humour and character to the stage; and as time went on, the sense of his past discouragements grew fainter, while the success of *The Deserted Village* increased his importance as an author. Sentimentalism, in the meantime, had still a majority. Kelly, it is true, was now no longer to be feared. His sudden good fortune had swept him into the ranks of the party-writers, with the result that the damning of his next play, *A Word to the Wise*, had been exaggerated into a political necessity. But the school which he represented had been recruited by a much abler man, Richard Cumberland, and it was probably the favourable reception of Cumberland's *West Indian* that stimulated Goldsmith into striking one more blow for legitimate comedy. At all events, in the autumn of the year in which *The West Indian* was produced, he is hard at work in the lanes at Hendon and Edgware, "studying jests with a most tragical countenance" for a successor to *The Good-Natur'd Man*.

To the modern spectator of *She Stoops to Conquer*, with its unflagging humour and bustling action, it must seem almost inconceivable that its stage qualities can ever have been questioned. Yet questioned they undoubtedly were, and Goldsmith was spared none of his former humiliations. Even from the outset, all was against him. His differences with Garrick had long been adjusted, and the Drury Lane manager would now probably have accepted a new play from his pen, especially as that astute observer had already detected signs of a reaction in the public taste. But Goldsmith was morally bound to Colman and Covent Garden; and Colman, in whose hands he placed his manuscript, proved even more disheartening and unmanageable than Garrick had been in the past. Before he had come to his decision, the close of 1772 had arrived. Early in the following year, under the irritation of suspense and suggested amendments combined, Goldsmith hastily transferred his proposal to Garrick; but, by Johnson's advice, as hastily withdrew it. Only by the express interposition of Johnson was Colman at last induced to make a distinct promise to bring out the play at a specific date. To believe in it, he could not be persuaded, and his contagious anticipations of its failure passed insensibly to the actors, who, one after the other, shuffled out of their parts. Even over the epilogue there were vexatious disputes, and when at last, in March, 1773, *She Stoops to Conquer* was acted, its *jeune premier* had previously held no more exalted position than that of ground-harlequin, while one of its most prominent characters had simply been a post-boy in *The Good-Natur'd Man*. But once fairly upon the boards neither lukewarm actors nor an adverse manager had any further influence over it, and the doubts of everyone vanished in the uninterrupted applause of the audience. When, a few days later, it was printed with a brief and grateful dedication to its best friend, Johnson, the world already knew with certainty that a fresh masterpiece had been added to the roll of English Dramatic Literature, and that " genteel comedy " had received a decisive blow.

The effect of this blow, it must be admitted, had been aided not a little by the appearance, only a week or two earlier, of Foote's clever puppet-show of *The Handsome Housemaid; or, Piety in Pattens*, which was openly directed at Kelly and his following. But ridicule by itself, without some sample of a worthier substitute, could not have sufficed to displace a persistent fashion. This timely antidote *She Stoops to Conquer*, in the most unmistakable way, afforded. From end to end of the piece there is not a sickly or a maudlin word. Even Sheridan, writing *The Rivals* two years later, thought it politic to insert " Faulkland " and " Julia " for the benefit of the sentimentalists. Goldsmith made no such concession, and his wholesome hearty merriment put to flight the Comedy of Tears,—even as the Coqcigrues vanished before the large-lunged laugh of Pantagruel. If, as Johnson feared, his plot bordered slightly upon farce—and of what good comedy may this not be said?—at least it can be urged that its most farcical incident, the mistaking of a gentleman's house for an inn, had really happened, since it had happened to the writer himself. But the superfine objections of Walpole and his friends are now ancient history,—history so ancient that it is scarcely credited, while Goldsmith's manly assertion (after Fielding) of the author's right " to stoop among the low to copy nature," has been ratified by successive generations of novelists and playwrights. What is beyond dispute is the healthy

atmosphere, the skilful setting, the lasting freshness and fidelity to human nature of the persons of
his drama. Not content with the finished portraits
of the Hardcastles (a Vicar and Mrs. Primrose
promoted to the squirearchy),—not content with
the incomparable and unapproachable Tony, the
author has managed to make attractive what is
too often insipid, his heroines and their lovers.
Miss Hardcastle and Miss Neville are not only
charming young women, but charming characters,
while Marlow and Hastings are much more than
stage young men. And let it be remembered—it
cannot be too often remembered—that in return-
ing to those Farquhars and Vanbrughs " of the
last age," who differed so widely from the Kellys
and Cumberlands of his own, Goldsmith has
brought back no taint of their baser part. Depending solely for its avowed intention to " make an
audience merry," upon the simple development of
its humorous incident, his play (wonderful to
relate!) attains its end without resorting to impure
suggestion or equivocal intrigue. Indeed, there is
but one married woman in the piece, and she
traverses it without a stain upon her character.

She Stoops to Conquer is Goldsmith's last
dramatic work, for the trifling sketch of *The
Grumbler* had never more than a grateful purpose.
When, only a year later, the little funeral procession from 2 Brick Court laid him in his unknown
grave in the Temple burying-ground, the new
comedy of which he had written so hopefully

to Garrick was still non-existent. Would it have been better than its last fortunate predecessor?—would those early reserves of memory and experience have still proved inexhaustible? The question cannot be answered. Through debt, and drudgery, and depression, the writer's genius had still advanced, and these might yet have proved powerless to check his progress. But at least it was given to him to end upon his best, and not to outlive it. For, in that critical sense which estimates the value of a work by its excellence at all points, it can scarcely be contested that *She Stoops to Conquer* is his best production. In spite of their beauty and humanity, the lasting quality of *The Traveller* and *The Deserted Village* is seriously prejudiced by his half-way attitude between the poetry of convention and the poetry of nature—between the gradus epithet of Pope and the direct vocabulary of Wordsworth. With *The Vicar of Wakefield*, again, immortal though it be, it is less his art that holds us, than his charm, his humour and his tenderness which tempt us to forget his inconsistency and his errors of haste. In *She Stoops to Conquer*, neither defect of art nor defect of nature forbids us to give unqualified admiration to a work which lapse of time has shown to be still unrivalled in its kind.

A TRANSLATOR OF PLATO'S "REPUBLIC"

By Richard Garnett

THE greatest authors of the world have bestowed
a portion of their immortality upon legions of
translators and commentators, parasite growths
which, in default of such stems to cling to, would
hardly have risen above the common level. It is
the special distinction of Plato to have been thus
ministered to by men of real genius, who, even
were everything they accomplished for him effaced
from the roll of their achievements, would still
have left very considerable names. Passing over
the Plotinus and Proclus of antiquity, and the
Pletho and Ficinus of the Renaissance, we find
this eminently true of those illustrious moderns,
Schleiermacher, Victor Cousin, and Benjamin
Jowett. If all the labours upon Plato which formed
so conspicuous a part of these distinguished men's
performance could be obliterated, their names
would still endure; but conversely, these would
be sufficiently preserved by their work on Plato
had they no other title to perpetuity: and, in
estimating their claims on the gratitude of posterity, their service to Plato occurs most readily
to the mind. Homer and Aristotle, Dante and

Shakespeare, have had more numerous disciples and apostles, but it is Plato's special glory to have attracted so many men of genius.

That service to Plato, nevertheless, is no sure passport to immortality is evinced by the complete oblivion which has overtaken the translation of Plato's *Republic*, by Dr. Harry Spens, although its priority to all other English translations, had it no other claim, should have kept it in remembrance. Published in 1763 at the Press of the University of Glasgow, by Foulis, the most eminent Scotch printer of the age, and dedicated to the Prime Minister, it appears to have attracted no notice from contemporaries, and has never been reprinted until now. The translator's own person is shrouded in almost equal obscurity. Though of sufficient consideration to fill the highest office to which a clergyman of the Church of Scotland can be called, he did not occupy any prominent position in the public eye, and the translation of the *Republic* appears to have been his solitary publication. The few particulars to be gleaned are chiefly official, and we are indebted for them to the research most obligingly made by Mr. J. Maitland Anderson, Librarian of the University of St. Andrews.

Spens, it appears, was the son of James Spens, Writer to the Signet, and was born in 1713 or 1714 at Kirkton, Alves, Elginshire, where his father possessed a landed estate which had been in the family for generations, which he transmitted to his son. Spens was educated at King's College and the University, Aberdeen, where he graduated M.A. in 1730. He was licensed to preach in 1738, was ordained minister of Wemyss, Fifeshire, in 1744, and received the degree of D.D. from the University of Aberdeen in 1761. In 1771 he married Anne Duncan. On December 29, 1779, he was installed Professor of Divinity in St. Mary's College, University of St. Andrews, and on May 25, 1780, received the high distinction of being elected Moderator of the General Assembly of the Church of Scotland. He died on November 27, 1787, leaving no family.

The following specimens will admit of a comparison being made between Spens and more recent translators who have wrought by a higher standard and enjoyed greater advantages. The examples are taken from Book III.

The judge, friend, governs the soul by the soul; which, if from its childhood it hath been educated with bad souls, and hath been conversant with them, and hath itself done all manner of evil, it is not able to come out from among them so as accurately, by itself, to judge of the evils of others, as happens in the diseases of the body; but it must, in its youth, be unexperienced and unpolluted with evil manners, if it means to be good and beautiful itself, and to judge soundly of what is just. And hence the virtuous, in their youth, appear simple, and easily deceived by the unjust, as they have not within themselves dispositions similar to those of the wicked.—*Spens*.

A juror, my friend, governs mind by mind; his mind, therefore, cannot be suffered to be reared from a tender age among vicious minds, and to associate with them, and to run the whole round of crimes in its own experience, in order to be quick in inferring the guilt of others from its own self-knowledge, as is allowable in the case of bodily disorders: on the contrary, it ought from his early youth to have been free from all experience and taint of evil habits, if it is to be qualified by its own thorough excellence to administer sound justice. And this is the reason why good men, when young, appear to be simple and easy victims to the impositions of bad men, because they have not in their own consciousness examples of like passions with the wicked.—*Davies and Vaughan.*

But with the judge it is otherwise, since he governs mind by mind; he ought not therefore to have been trained among vicious minds, and to have associated with them from his youth upwards, and to have gone through the whole calendar of crime, only that he may quickly infer the crimes of others as he might their bodily diseases from his own self-consciousness; the honourable mind which is to form a healthy judgment shall have had no experience or contamination of evil habits when young. And this is the reason why in youth good men often appear to be simple, and are easily practised upon by the dishonest, because they have no examples of what evil is in their own souls.—*Jowett.*

These translations, it will be seen, agree in substance, but Spens has gone wrong in deeming that Plato admits the possibility of the magistrate having been brought up in iniquity, which Plato refuses to contemplate; and is evidently quite astray as to the connection of διεξεληλυθέναι, which he refers to the company of the wicked, instead of the practice of wickedness.

On the whole, Spens's version should not be lightly esteemed. It is clearly the work of a scholar and a man of considerable literary ability, who might have rivalled his successors if the standard of his age had been higher, and if he had possessed the *apparatus criticus* at their disposal. They had magnificent libraries at their command, which gave access to a mass of Platonic literature which did not exist in his day. His labours suffer much in comparison by the absence of the illuminating comment which imparts such zest to the versions of Davies and of Jowett. This arises in great measure from their special attention to the needs of students, while Spens considers only the general reader, who, by a pleasing fiction, was supposed to be able to read Plato without note or comment.

The long disquisition upon Plato which Spens has prefixed to his translation is eminently characteristic of the eighteenth century, elegant in diction, philanthropic in intention, and devoid of real grasp or insight. It neither throws nor endeavours to throw any new light upon Plato himself: his reputation is taken for granted, and it is supposed that his " sentiments " will be sufficiently ascertained from the perusal of his treatise. This, in the translator's as in Rousseau's opinion, is a treatise on justice, and Plato's commonwealth is merely projected as an illustration of his principles in action, " supposing the most perfect form of civil government to be an image and representation of that internal constitution and government formed and established by nature in the mind of a good man." Something like an analysis is attempted, but the delicate question of the community of women is evaded. Indeed, the translator lays more stress upon his second object, " to stir up the English youth to the study of the ancients," not Plato only. He deplores the decay of the taste for ancient literature, and agrees with almost all contemporary writers in lamenting the luxury of the age, and the universal propensity to read for mere amusement. The perusal of the *Republic*, he deems, may allure the thoughtless reader: " It is handled in an elegant manner, and many things collateral and in connection with the principal subject are most delicately touched; so that the reader is perpetually delighted with the variety of the matter, the beauty of the illustrations, the union of the whole, and, in particular, with that genuine air of real life which everywhere appears." If any ancient writer, then, can be read in the eighteenth century Plato will be. Spens's version has been so little heard of that it is much to be feared that its reception cannot have justified his anticipations. The dedication to Lord Bute, exempt from servility as it is, would not at that juncture recommend it to any but North Britons, and it may probably have been little heard of south of the Tweed. It merited a better fate as the first English translation, as a courageous undertaking carried out with exemplary diligence;

and also from the amiable character of the translator, who reveals himself as a man of broad if nowise original mind, the warm admirer of Bacon and Newton and Hoadly, and endowed with such candour as to bestow the most cordial applause upon Sydenham's translation of Plato. This never reached the *Republic*, and Spens remained without a competitor until the publication of Thomas Taylor's version in 1804. He does not say how long his work had occupied him, but intimates that he had used no other translator or commentator than Ficinus.

The *Republic* of Plato deserves an eminent place among the epoch-making books of the world. It was probably the first in which full expression was given to the longing which must of necessity arise in the human heart when the cosmos and the individual appear at odds, so tersely expressed in Fitzgerald's *Omar Khayyám*—

Ah Love! could you and I with Fate conspire
To grasp this sorry Scheme of Things entire,
  Would we not shatter it to bits—and then
Re-mould it nearer to the Heart's Desire?

In estimating the *Republic's* place in the history of thought we must take into account the circumstances under which it was composed. The exact date is uncertain, but whether it existed in the form of a book by 393 B.C. or not, its ideals certainly then existed in Plato's mind and were known to his fellow-citizens, for the community of goods and the community of women are ridiculed in the *Ecclesiazusæ* of Aristophanes, acted in that year. As a young man Plato had passed through terrible experiences, the complete shipwreck of the vessel of State by the disastrous termination of the Peloponnesian War, the atrocities of the oligarchical party who thereupon gained dominion in Athens, and the unjust execution of his own adored master by an ignorant and misguided democracy. Such events were well calculated to engender in Plato's mind a distrust of all existing political systems, and to set him upon seriously projecting something to replace them. Ever since, the creation of ideal communities has been the frequent amusement of superior minds, and although every such endeavour has but strengthened the conviction that, as a matter of fact, the development of society must proceed upon the lines marked out for it from the beginning, in these, nevertheless, the aspiration after something

> Too bright and good
> For human nature's daily food

is no unimportant factor. The winged genius which in ancient works of art accompanies the chariot of hero or demi-god adds nothing to the power or the speed, but stimulates the ardour of the charioteer.

Plato is broadly distinguished from his successors, More, Campanella, Bacon, Brockden Brown, etc., and his later self in his *Critias*, in this respect, that whereas these represent their ideal communities as already existing and only needing to be described, his Republic exists merely in thought, and not even there until it has been provided with a sound basis by a preliminary discussion of the abstract principles of justice.

"Nothing actually existing in the world," says Jowett, "at all resembles Plato's ideal State, nor does he himself imagine that such a State is possible." This he repeats in the *Laws* (Book V.) where, casting a glance back on the *Republic*, he admits that the perfect state of communism and philosophy was impossible in his own age, though still to be retained as a pattern. When asked how the ideal polity can come into being, he answers ironically, "When one son of a king becomes a philosopher." It is worthy of note, however, that, little more than a century before Plato wrote, a son of a king *had* become a philosopher—Buddha.

We know not whether any commentator has noticed the resemblance between the prisoners in the seventh book of the *Republic*, who see only shadows cast upon the wall of their dungeon from the road adjoining, to the Lady of Shalott,—

> Shining through a mirror clear
> That hangs before her all the year,
> Shadows of the world appear:
> There she sees the highway near,
>   Winding down to Camelot.

Was Tennyson conscious of the parallel with Plato when, in *The Palace of Art*, he places along with "large-brow'd Verulam" first among *i maestri*

di color che sanno? This dignity Dante confines
to Aristotle; but Aristotle was the Doctor of the
rival University, and the proud position assigned
to Bacon is probably less a compliment to him
than to his editor, Tennyson's friend Spedding.

The only personal notice of Spens to be met
with is highly to his credit. The Rev. James
Hall, in his *Travels in Scotland* (1807), describes
him as "amiable, polite, and accomplished," and
further as hitherto the only minister who had
been able to instil some notion of religion into
the people of Buckhaven, who must have been
under his pastoral charge when he was minister
of Wemyss. These people were of Danish race,
descendants of a shipload of Danish fishers of both
sexes driven ashore about the beginning of the
eighteenth century, and who in Spens's time still
followed the fisherman's calling. Suspicions of
their neighbours and the idea that they were
ridiculed by them had kept them strangers in
such a state of isolation that religion and civilisation had nearly died out among them; and,
though they spoke the language of the country,
Spens found his instructions totally unintelligible.
Proceeding, however, from objects and ideas that
were familiar to their minds to others with which
they were unacquainted, but to which those
familiar ideas bore some resemblance or analogy,
Dr. Spens succeeded in communicating some
notions of a Creator, a Redeemer, and a future
judgment. The obstacles he had to encounter in

this pious and laudable work, and the means by which he surmounted them, suggested " a subject of philosophical speculation to the worthy and ingenious doctor, who would sometimes amuse his friends with an account of both."

HUGH LATIMER

By Henry Charles Beeching

LATIMER is the best example the English Church can show of the popular preacher. The sermons of Andrewes or Donne make their appeal to a trained intelligence which can "divide," even to the last scruple, "the word of truth"; Latimer, whether he is preaching in a country town or before the king at Westminster, always speaks so that the servants and handmaids shall carry away as much as the gentler sort. He has but one subject, that of righteousness, and the appeal of righteousness is not to the intellect, but to the conscience.

This is not to say that Latimer himself was unlearned. As a young man he was elected fellow of his college (Clare Hall) at Cambridge, and was one of twelve preachers licensed by the University to preach in any part of England. When his university suspected him of the Lutheran heresy, and he was summoned before Wolsey, he is said to have shown himself more at home in Duns Scotus than Wolsey's chaplains, who were set to examine him. It is probable that he was not deeply versed in the New Learning, being born a little too early for that. The year 1510, in which

Erasmus went to Cambridge to teach Greek, was the year in which Latimer took his degree, and we know that at first the new professor found but few pupils.

The story of Latimer's first attraction to the Reformed doctrines is told by himself in the first sermon on the Lord's Prayer:

Master Bilney, or rather Saint Bilney, that suffered death for God's word sake, the same Bilney was the instrument whereby God called me to knowledge; for I may thank him, next to God, for that knowledge that I have in the word of God. For I was as obstinate a papist as any was in England, insomuch that when I should be made bachelor of divinity, my whole oration went against Philip Melanchthon and against his opinions. Bilney heard me at that time, and perceived that I was zealous without knowledge; and he came to me afterward in my study and desired me, for God's sake, to hear his confession. I did so: and, to say the truth, by his confession I learned more than before in many years. So from that time forward I began to smell the word of God, and forsook the school-doctors and such fooleries.

This was in 1524, and already the next year we find that he had become suspected of favouring what in his bachelor's thesis he had attacked; for his diocesan, Bishop West of Ely, came up " suddenly and secretly " to Cambridge to hear a Latin sermon he was to preach *ad clerum*, and entered the church with unepiscopal astuteness after the sermon was begun. But for once the greatest diplomatist of his age was overmatched. With extraordinary readiness Latimer changed his text, and preached a sermon extempore from the text *Christus existens Pontifex futurorum bonorum.* "A new auditory requireth a new theme, therefore it behoveth me to entreat of the honourable office of a bishop." The bishop thanked Latimer for his "good sermon," and asked him to preach against Martin Luther's doctrine. To which Latimer very fairly replied that he could not refute what he was prohibited from reading. It is ill setting one's wits against authority; and according to Cranmer's secretary Morice, from whom this story comes, the bishop, who had the last word, replied, "I perceive that you somewhat smell of the pan, Mr. Latymer; you will repent this gear some day." He was inhibited by the bishop from preaching in the university, but continued to use the church of the Austin Friars, which was extra-diocesan. It was on occasion of this dispute that Wolsey interfered and had Latimer examined, with the result that he licensed him to preach anywhere in England.

Of the Cambridge period we have two sermons preserved, those on the Card, preached about 1529, which raise the question what it was that the Bishop of Ely and the party of the Old Learning found to complain of in Latimer's preaching. The answer of course is that here, as in all theological controversies, it was not the heresy, but the heretic, that was attacked. The sermons only "smelt of the pan." They disparaged "voluntary works" —church-building, pilgrimages, gilding of saints, and so forth, not absolutely, but in comparison with " necessary works " of righteousness and mercy. Still it is not prudent for the clergy to disparage works of popular religion. Responsible rulers must " doubt whereunto this will grow." The conceit of comparing the Commandments to playing-cards is not to our modern taste; but Latimer was wise in his generation and knew what he was doing. Probably by such a trick he caught the ear of the undergraduates of the day, who were younger then than now. It is interesting to compare these early sermons of Latimer's with the almost contemporary sermons of Bishop Fisher. In reading Fisher there rises to memory the wonderfully beautiful and suffering face that we know from Holbein's drawing, a face that is certainly not of the world. And the sermons also are not of the world. They are full of a sense of the hollowness of all earthly satisfaction; but they do not strike us as showing any acquaintance at first hand with what they despise and renounce. In one place, for example, commenting on the text " Can a woman forget her sucking child ? " Fisher lays down that " the affection of fathers is longer-during than that of mothers." Throughout we feel the lessons to be a little too abstract, the similies a little forced, the examples conventional; although there is no mistaking the passion of the preacher. Now, whatever we may think of Latimer's divinity, about his humanity there can be no manner of doubt. From the first his sermons

display a quite remarkable insight into the work-
ing of the human mind and will. In the second
Sermon on the Card, on the words, " Go first and
reconcile thy neighbour," he has this penetrating
counsel:

Be not ashamed to do thy Master's and Lord's
will and commandment. Go, as I said, unto thy
neighbour that is offended by thee, and reconcile
him whom thou hast lost by thy unkind words, by
thy scorns, mocks, and other disdainous words and
behaviours, and be not nice to ask of him the cause
why he is displeased with thee: require of him
charitably to remit; and cease not till you both
depart, one from the other, true brethren in Christ.
Come not to thy neighbour whom thou hast offended,
and give him a pennyworth of ale, or a banquet, and
so make him a fair countenance, thinking that by
thy drink or dinner he will shew thee like countenance. I grant you may both laugh and make
good cheer, and yet there may remain a bag of rusty
malice, twenty years old, in thy neighbour's bosom.

The topic which aroused the bitter resentment
of his clerical brethren, the disparagement of
voluntary works, introduced into this sermon as
an illustration of the text "Leave there thy ob-
lation," forms no small part of Latimer's practical
teaching from first to last. He saw that religion
had come to be identified in the popular mind
with certain observances, none of which had any
necessary connection with the " weightier matters
of the law." As against this view of religion, as a
system of merely ecclesiastical duties, he is always
endeavouring to recall men's interest to the funda-
mental verities of righteousness and mercy.

While they thus preached to the people, that dead images not only ought to be covered with gold, but also ought of all faithful and christian people (yea, in this scarceness and penury of all things), to be clad with silk garments, and those also laden with precious gems and jewels; and to be lighted with wax candles, as who should say, here no cost can be too great; whereas in the meantime we see Christ's faithful and lively images, bought with no less price than with his most precious blood (alas, alas!), to be an-hungered, a-thirst, a-cold, and to lie in darkness, wrapped in all wretchedness, yea, to lie there till death take away their miseries.[1]

For a while after his triumph over the Bishop of Ely Latimer's enemies had to possess their souls in patience, because, having taken the king's side in the matter of the divorce, he was in high favour at court. He was one of twelve Cambridge divines appointed with twelve from Oxford as a Royal Commission to examine heretical books. Among the books they condemned was Tyndale's Bible. The accession of Anne Boleyn brought him the bishopric of Worcester, which he held for four years; doing his best during that period for the reform of abuses, especially making a crusade against the popular images—" our great Sibyl, with her old sister of Walsingham, her young sister of Ipswich, with their two other sisters of Doncaster and Penrice," but resigning his see when the Statute of the Six Articles was passed (1539), which made him a heretic. It is said that the king saved him from the stake only on the direct

---

[1] Sermon before the Convocation, 1536.

intercession of Cromwell. But even when highest in favour he must have realised, as every good man who served the king had sooner or later to realise, how little the Supreme Head of the Church of Christ in England cared for the lives of any of its members. As early as 1531, and again in 1532, he was accused of heresy in Convocation; and though he appealed to the king, Henry refused to interfere, and Latimer escaped the heretic's fate only by a full recantation. Among the articles he was compelled to sign are such as these: There is a place of purgatory. Souls in purgatory are helped by masses and alms-deeds. Pilgrimages and oblations are meritorious. It is profitable to invocate saints. Images are profitable. It is profitable for them to be decked and trimmed and to have candles set before them. His opinion on these matters is well set out in a letter to Archbishop Warham of the same year: " I have never preached anything contrary to the truth, nor contrary to the decrees of the Fathers, nor as far as I know contrary to the Catholic faith. I have desired, I own, and do desire, a reformation in the judgment of the vulgar, *that they should distinguish between duties*; that all men should know that there is a very great difference between those works which God hath prepared for each of us (zealously discharging the duties of our respective callings) to walk in, and those that are voluntary, which we undertake by our own state and pleasure. It is lawful, I own, to make use of images, to go on pilgrimage, to pray to saints, to be mindful of souls abiding in purgatory; but these things, which are voluntary, are to be so moderated that God's commandments of necessary obligation, which bring eternal life to those that keep them, and eternal death to those that neglect them, be not deprived of their just value." The only one of these topics that calls for any particular comment is that of purgatory: what was Latimer's belief about it? Latimer's attack upon purgatory took the form, at first and in the main, of denying the Pope's claim to deliver from it, which had been made so profitable a source of revenue. He calls it, again and again, " purgatory pick-purse." It was only by degrees that he came to renounce a belief in purgatory altogether, and even in his latest sermons he is not consistent with himself. In one he says distinctly, " You must understand that there are but two places appointed of Almighty God for all mankind, that is, heaven and hell "; [1] in another he allows that he did not know the answer to the question where the soul of the young maid, the ruler's daughter, was, after it went out of her; " but where it pleased God it should be, there it was. If the Bishop of Rome had gone no further we should have been well enough." [2] His earlier view is well set out in the answer he drew up to some articles " untruly, unjustly, falsely, uncharitably imputed to me by

[1] Sermon on Fifth Sunday after Epiphany, Feb. 1552.
[2] Sermon of same year.

Dr. Powell of Salisbury." [1] One of these articles
is that " there is no purgatory after this life."
This Latimer shows to have been a misunder-
standing; his doctrine had been that the souls in
purgatory have less need of our prayers, as being
" always in charity," than we have of theirs. " We
may well pray for them, and they much better
for us; which they will do of their charity, though
we desire them not." But the conclusion of the
whole matter for him was that too much attention
to souls in purgatory, " who are in God's favour
and have Christ with them," diverted attention
from souls on earth, who might be in extreme
necessity.

We see not who needeth in purgatory; but we see
who needeth in this world. And John saith, " If thou
see thy brother, and help him not, how is the charity
of God in thee?" Here we be bound to help one
another, as we would be holpen ourselves, under pain
of damnation. Here, for lack of help, we may murmur
and grudge against God, dishonour God, foredote
ourselves: which inconveniences shall not follow if
we do our duty one to another. I am sure the souls
in purgatory be so charitable, and of charity so loth
to have God dishonoured, that they would have
nothing withdrawn from the poor here in this world

---

[1] Dr. Powell, prebendary of Salisbury, a theologian of
great learning, who had been engaged by the king to
write against Luther, had preached, with others, against
Latimer for his sermons at Bristol in 1533. A commission
was appointed to inquire into the dispute, and Dr. Powell
was sent to the Tower. He was executed in 1540, among
that famous six at Smithfield, three hanged, drawn, and
quartered for treason, in denying the king's supremacy,
and three burned for heresy.

to be bestowed upon them. Therefore, howsoever we do for purgatory, let us provide to keep out of hell. I would have difference betwixt that that *may* be done, and that that *ought* to be done; and this to go before that, and that to come after this.

When Protestantism was set up with the accession of Edward VI., Latimer did not return to his bishopric, but lodged with Cranmer at Lambeth, and devoted himself to preaching. His Swiss servant Bernher, who edited some of his sermons, tells us that he preached twice every Sunday during King Edward's reign. The first of these sermons, "preached in the Shrouds at Paul's Cross," *i.e.* in a sheltered place where the sermons were given in bad weather, is the only one that has survived of a course on "the Plough." It is mainly directed against "unpreaching prelates," and contains the memorable saying that the devil is "never out of his diocese."

"*Circuit*," he goeth about in every corner of his diocese: he goeth on visitation daily: he leaveth no place of his cure unvisited; he walketh round about from place to place, and ceaseth not.

But the sermon contains one passage which was to be the precursor of many such in future—a cry to London to repent of its covetousness. "Charity is waxen cold, none helpeth the scholar nor yet the poor." In the first sermon of the Lent following, preached before the king, he returns to the subject in regard to rural England. The dissolution of the monasteries had meant the destruction of the monastic schools, with their free education. It had meant also the transference of the manors to lay landlords who were disposed to exact the uttermost farthing of rent; and also to enclose the commons. Moreover, the development of the wool trade encouraged them to lay down their estates in pasture; and this threw a large number of the labourers out of employment, and filled the towns with beggars. On all these topics —upon which, himself the son of a Leicestershire yeoman, he could speak from experience—Latimer probes the consciences of his courtly hearers. In these sermons before King Edward we have one of the most vivid pictures of the age. Here, for example, is a striking contrast between the old times and the new:

My father was a yeoman, and had no lands of his own, only he had a farm of three or four pound by year at the uttermost, and hereupon he tilled so much as kept half a dozen men. He had walk for a hundred sheep; and my mother milked thirty kine. He was able, and did find the king a harness, with himself and his horse. . . . He kept me to school, or else I had not been able to have preached before the king's majesty now. He married my sisters with five pound or twenty nobles apiece; so that he brought them up in godliness and fear of God. He kept hospitality for his poor neighbours, and some alms he gave to the poor. And all this he did of the said farm, where he that now hath it payeth sixteen pound by year, or more, and is not able to do anything for his prince, for himself, nor for his children, or give a cup of drink to the poor.

On one topic, as became his office, Latimer was

urgent: that maintenance should be found for poor scholars at school and the universities, so that they might recruit the ranks of the preachers. "Is this realm," he asks, "taught by rich men's sons? No, no, read the Chronicles. Ye shall find sometime noblemen's sons which have been unpreaching bishops and prelates: but . . . by yeomen's sons the faith of Christ is, and hath been, maintained chiefly." The name of Edward VI. is still held in pious memory for the schools he founded; but it is forgotten that those he founded, or refounded, were but a fraction of those that were suppressed by the merciless confiscation of the property of the Guilds. Preaching at Stamford in 1550, Latimer says: "To consider that hath been plucked from abbeys, colleges, and chantries, it is marvel no more to be bestowed upon this holy office of salvation. Schools are not maintained; scholars have not exhibition; the preaching office decayeth." And he asks his hearers, in another place, "to bestow as much in the feeding of scholars of good wits, of poor men's sons, as ye were wont to bestow in pilgrimage matters, in trentals, in masses, in pardons, in purgatory matters."

But not only do agriculture and education come within the scope of this denouncer of covetousness; he has a word for the judge who takes bribes: and having in the third sermon before King Edward told the tale of Cambyses flaying an unjust judge and covering the judgment seat with his skin, he recurs to this again and again.

"It were a goodly sign, this of the judge's skin. I pray God we may once see the sign of the skin in England." He has a word also for the receiver of fraudulent commissions, and the adulterating manufacturer. On the text "Thy wine is mingled with water" he comments: "Here he meddleth with vintners; belike there were brewers in those days as there be now. . . . I hear say there is a certain cunning come up in mixing of wares. How say you? were it no wonder to hear that cloth-makers should become poticaries? Yea, and (as I hear say) in such a place, where as they have professed the gospel and the word of God most earnestly of a long time." And he goes on to explain the mystery of flock-powder. To all classes he is a faithful monitor. "The servant who has his whole wages and does but half his work, or is a sluggard, that same fellow is a thief before God." The fearlessness of Latimer was one of his marked characteristics. The man who had his trunk packed ready to start when the pursuivant came to summon him to a trial that could have no issue but the stake was not the man to be daunted by kings or mobs. When he first came into favour with Henry VIII. by his judgment about the divorce, and thus for a moment quieted his enemies, the first thing he must do is to re-monstrate with the king in a Lent sermon for ordering that his horses should be pastured on abbey lands, "abbeys being ordained for the comfort of the poor." His sermon before the

Convocation of 1536, of which we have only a translation, recalls in its boldness the great sermon of Colet, a quarter of a century before. He said as strong things many times afterwards about unpreaching prelates; but that was in the reign of Edward, when he was safe. Under Henry he was never safe.

There is no need to make the attempt to sum up Latimer's characteristics as a preacher. A single page of any sermon shows the whole man, in his simplicity, his directness, his burning zeal, his humanity, his quaint terms, his garrulousness. His sermons were talked; and as they were expected to last for a couple of hours, humorous relief was very welcome to both preacher and hearer. No preacher had so inexhaustible a stock of merry tales—not the cut-and-dried moralised anecdotes of the *Gesta Romanorum*, but incidents that he had noted in his busy life among the people. A good example will be found in the third sermon before Edward VI. Now and then he does not disdain what we should call a " Joe Miller," as when he tells of the gentlewoman who went to St. Thomas of Acres to the sermon, because she " never failed of a good nap there." Frequently he illustrates from his own personal history—as the question of giving tribute to Cæsar, by an examination he had to undergo before the bishop. If the modern reader is inclined to resent the occasional homeliness of the vocabulary as beneath the dignity of the pulpit—as when it is said that the covetous man's mind is "on his half-penny"; or when the preacher quotes a proverb "of my country: They say when they call the hogs to the swine-trough, 'Come to thy mingle-mangle, come pur, come pur'"; or when he paraphrases *Num et vos seducti estis?* by "What, ye brain-sick fools, ye hoddy-pecks, ye doddy-pouls, ye huddes, are you seduced also?"—it is well to remember that the final cause of the pulpit is not the dignity of the preacher, but the instruction of the hearer, and that before a man can hear he must be drawn to listen. Moreover, in these days of universal education we cannot appreciate the ignorance of the simple people in Latimer's day. It may be brought home to us by the concluding passage of the sermon at Stamford in which Latimer tells us that he made a habit of reciting the Lord's Prayer before and after every sermon, as he found so many poor people did not know it.

THE POETS' POET

By John W. Hales

Largely as Spenser borrowed in *The Faerie Queene* from books—especially from the Classics and from the Italians—it is clear that he borrowed yet more largely from contemporary society and history, and that he mirrors in it the events and the personages of his own age. But, of course, such historical interpretations are quite distinct from poetical studies. Obviously, the first duty of a poem is to be poetical, not historical, or ethical, or metaphysical.

Beyond question, what moved Spenser to write was a genuine poetic impulse. As we have seen, his mind was indeed profoundly interested in the great movements of his time; he was a thoroughly intelligent and devoted Protestant; he admired and cultivated "the new learning" with rare ability and fervent delight; he was penetrated and pervaded by a passionate patriotism. But in addition to all these incitements and motives he was actuated by a real creative instinct. He sang because he must, not only because people listened, and there was so much to say. His heart was hot within him; and while he was thus musing, the fire kindled, and at the last he "spake with his tongue." He sang, not because he was learned—an epithet often assigned him by his contemporaries — or an intense votary of the Reformation or the Renascence, but because his imagination longed for outward embodiment, because it must needs give birth to its divine conceptions, because it insisted on relief and deliverance. In other words, Spenser's poetry is a true incarnation of a poetical spirit, not the elaborate effort of a partisan, literary, political, religious.

It is his inexhaustible freshness and abundance of fancy, combined with his astonishing dominion over language and over rime and rhythm, that has won for Spenser his distinguishing title of "the Poets' Poet." The material he uses is sometimes prosaic enough, as especially in the Second Book, in his description of the House of Alma, otherwise the human body, or in his versification of Geoffrey of Monmouth's *History of the Britons* in the following Canto; but under any and all circumstances, whether he is happy in his immediate subject or not, whatever are the strange tasks he sets himself, or ponderous burdens he undertakes, he never ceases to be a poet, and it can never be forgotten by any capable and appreciative reader that he is a poet. In most great poets there is a certain vein of prose which "crops up" from time to time. No one is wise at all hours, says an old Latin adage; certainly, it is true that no one is poetical at all hours. Instead of flying and soaring according to their proper form of movement, we see poets walking, or even crawling, *i.e.*, their speech, in Horace's phrase, becomes "pedestrian." Now, whatever may be Spenser's deficiencies and faults, it seems true that no one ever lived more constantly and fully in the world of imagination than he, —that, though others may have risen higher, no one ever sank out of his empyrean and touched the gross earth less frequently or fatally. "Of all the poets," writes Hazlitt, "he is the most poetical." Whatever we may think of his Fairy land in other respects, there can be no question that it is a province of poetry.

Spenser created a new world, which, from its first appearance in the firmament of literature, had a special charm and fascination for his brother artists, who, generation after generation, delighted to wander in it.

There are several traces in Shakespeare's Plays of his familiarity with Spenser's Poems, and personally they must have been well acquainted, meeting often no doubt at the house of their common friend Lord Essex. Not, however, to insist on imperfectly ascertained relations, no less a person than Milton declared Spenser was his "poetical father"; and without any such declaration we should confidently have interred this spiritual sonship, so evident is Spenser's influence on Milton's earlier poetry. In the *Areopagitica* also

Milton speaks of "our sage and serious Spenser whom I dare be known to think a better teacher than Scotus and Aquinas." Dryden and Pope are by no means poets of the Spenserian type; yet both of them testify their debt and their admiration. With the revival of the imagination in the last century arose a yet warmer enthusiasm for Spenser. Thomson's lines in his *Summer* are highly appreciative as well as discriminating:

> Nor shall my verse that elder bard forget,
> The gentle Spenser, Fancy's pleasing son,
> Who, like a copious river, pour'd his song
> O'er all the mazes of enchanted ground.

Certainly on what is best of Thomson's work, as on *The Castle of Indolence*, the influence of Spenser is very deeply impressed. Gray found the perusal of Spenser one of his best incentives and excitements, when he wished to cultivate the poetical mood. The air of *The Faerie Queene* seemed to arouse and invigorate his often languid faculties. To Wordsworth, Byron, Shelley, Keats, that same air was scarcely less delightful and scarcely less benign.

Amongst our poets Wordsworth was perhaps one of the least susceptible to literary impressions; and yet we see with what grateful joy he submitted himself to the sweet influence of Spenser. Probably the first lines Keats wrote were headed *In imitation of Spenser*. Possibly the power of Spenser over him at that time was to a large extent indirect, that is, was exercised through intermediate writers; but to the end of his life, acting indirectly or directly, it was a determining force. A last century writer, one Dr. Sewell, made the memorable remark that "more poets have sprung from Spenser than all other English writers."

Thus, whatever Spenser's defects, however true it may be that he is wanting in humour, that in archaising his grammar and his vocabulary he "writ no language," that his characters lack at times human interest, and whatever else Zoiluses or even well-meaning and generous critics may urge against him, it remains that to highly sensitive natures he is a poet of exceptional and of sovereign charm, of an inspiration that is singularly full and overflowing, so that—

> Hither, as to their fountain, other stars
> Repairing in their urns draw golden light.

In spite of all his superabundance of fantasy, his want of human substance, and his epic confusions in *The Faerie Queene*, Spenser securely holds one of the chief thrones of English poetry; and around no one of our poetic kings is there gathered a court more remarkable for its selectness, its culture, and its devotion; and on him, as we have mentioned, has been conferred by right divine the significant "style" of the Poets' Poet. As we have seen, from Drayton and Raleigh and many another Elizabethan down to Wordsworth and Keats and many another singer of the nineteenth century, all the poets, with scarcely an exception, rise up and call him blessed. For three hundred years now he has been one of the supreme inspiring influences of our literature. If his work is not perfect, yet it suggests a sense of perfection, that is, it brings vividly before us one visited and possessed by visions of rare loveliness, and striving with no common cunning and no common success to embody them worthily and immortally. And, whatever its imperfections as a whole, it contains pictures and passages of incomparable finish and beauty, pictures and passages as nearly perfect as anything that has proceeded from human pen. "The heavenly Una with her milk-white lamb" will remain to the end of time one of the fairest and sweetest figures to be found in books. He who could create so exquisite a being was unquestionably and beyond all protest an artist of the highest order, even though he failed to accomplish any other like achievement. But indeed *The Faerie Queene* abounds in stanzas and in passages of surpassing beauty, and in signs and tokens of a nature haunted and inspired by the very spirit of grace and loveliness.

PRINTED BY
THE TEMPLE PRESS AT LETCHWORTH
IN GREAT BRITAIN